I0201227

# The
# Ohio Ministers Pulpit
# 2015

Compiled by
Dr. Alton E. Loveless

Copyright 2015
By
Dr. Alton E. Loveless
ISBN 978-1-940609-33-1

All rights reserved
No part of this book may be reproduced or transmitted in any form or by
any means, electronic or mechanical, including photocopying, recording,
or by any information storage and retrieval system, without permission
in writing from the copyright owner.
This book was printed in the United States of America.
To order additional copies of this book, contact:

FWB Publications
1006 Rayme Drive
Columbus, Ohio 43207
740--777-1944

Published by
FWB Publications

FWB

For many years I have listened to great preaching and have concluded the Ohio Free Will Baptist preachers are among some of the best I have heard during my 61 years of ministry.

I count it an honor to include of few messages from these men.

Alton E. Loveless

# Table of Contents

# 1

## Power under Control

Matthew 5:5

---

**Paul R. Etterling II**
Lead Pastor, Westerville Free Will Baptist

Frances and I were celebrating our anniversary. Kylie was attending an event with the youth group and Joel was with us. So, we decided to celebrate our anniversary by spending the day with him. What better thing to do on a cold and rainy October day than to go horseback riding? Frances had ridden before. Joel and I had not. So, this was sure to be a great experience.

The leader gave a few brief instructions on how to mount the horse, use the reins to control the horse and what to do if the horse decided to stop and eat something along the path. So far, all was good. My horses' name was Solomon. Solomon was a big horse. I suppose a big man requires a big horse. As I mounted him, the thought came to me, "You are in real trouble if this horse decides to do his own thing. Maybe, I should have worn one of those helmets that they offered me."

The ride up the hill and around the path began. For the most part, it was a very uneventful ride. Except that one moment when my life flashed before my eyes. We came to a place in the path where Solomon would step down a slight embankment and across a ditch. The problem was that as Solomon started across, he found a hedge apple that he wanted to eat. So, heading down hill across the embankment, he lowers his head all the way down into the ditch to get the hedge apple. I lost my balance and began to fall forward on him. It was at that moment I heard the leader say, "Kick and pull up." So, I did. After all, my life depended on it (or so I thought). It was amazing. As I kicked and pulled upward on the reins, Solomon dropped the hedge apple and finished crossing the ditch without incident.

As we were leaving the farm, another thought came to me, "How neat was it that Joel was able to control the horse he was riding?" Joel had just turned nine. Obviously, his horse was much smaller than mine. But, it was still big and powerful enough to hurt him if something went wrong. Yet, using the very same technique of holding the reins in his hand he was able to control the horse. That is a picture of meekness.

Meekness is power under control. Those very same horses that we rode that day could have been very destructive if they were wild. In the wild, horses often display power that is out of control. But trainers had worked with Solomon and the other horses to break and tame them. Solomon displayed power under control that day when I rode him. As a matter of fact, when an animal like a horse is broken and tamed, the power they possess can be productive rather than destructive. Solomon used his power that day to take me around the farm that would have otherwise taken a couple of hours to walk on my own. A farmer can break a horse and productively use the power of the horse in his farming. Sometimes, the police use horses to patrol an area or event. There are many ways that the power of a horse can be used productively when brought under control.

This is the very thing that Jesus spoke of when he said, "Blessed are the meek: for they shall inherit the earth." (Matthew 5:5) Jesus said this in the context of the Sermon on the Mount. He opens His sermon with short tweets as it were describing the characteristics of the Kingdom. There is a definite progression in Matthew 5:3-5: The person who recognizes their own spiritual bankruptcy will mourn and be broken over their own sin and the sin around them. This brokenness leads a person to meekness because he realizes that he can do nothing for himself.

This was shocking to the Jews. They were looking for a Messiah with a great kingdom. The idea of brokenness and meekness was not exactly how they would have characterized the kingdom they were looking for. This was not just shocking to them, but in all probability it was also scandalous. But, this is exactly what the kingdom of God looks like.

What does meekness look like for those who are living under the reign and rule of God in their lives? First, meekness is not weakness. Just as I described in the opening illustration meekness is the opposite of weakness. It is power under control. The person who is meek actually possesses more power than the one who is perceived as powerful by the standards of the world. Why? Because meekness is characterized by humility. May I remind you that no person ever becomes a follower of Jesus Christ in pride? Those who become His followers do so by repenting of their pride and approaching Him in humility. Also, meekness is not weakness because it is connected to gentleness in the Scriptures.

Gentleness is when you are in the restaurant and they completely mess up your order. You are not the one to cause a scene. But, you kindly and politely remind the server what you ordered. This happened to us recently in a restaurant. They did not completely mess up our order. But, the service was very slow. So, at the end of the dinner, Frances asked if she could speak to a manager. The manager came over and Frances politely explained to him what our experience was like that night. Of course, he went through the routine and offered to remove the specific items from the bill. Frances stopped him and said, "I am not telling you this because I want a free dinner. I ordered the dinner and I will pay for the dinner. But, I think that you and your employees need to know what our experience was like so that you can improve on these things." That is a gentle way of handling such a situation. A situation like that could have become very destructive if it had not been handled gently.

Secondly, meekness is not natural. Parents understand this. There are times when we find ourselves out of control in dealing with our children. Why? Because meekness is not natural. There is nothing in humanity that leads you to meekness. As a matter of fact, the Apostle Paul recognized that meekness is not natural when he listed it as one of the nine characteristics of the fruit of the Spirit. (Galatians 5:2)

Thirdly, this leads to the conclusion that meekness is dependent upon God. If you confess to be a follower of Jesus Christ, but you often find yourself out of control, then there is something wrong with your understanding of the life you have in Christ. To be meek means that you are not weak but it is also not natural to you. Therefore, you are dependent every moment of your life upon the Holy Spirit to work in you and through you to live in meekness. This is consistent with the opening statements of Jesus in His sermon as He describes the person who is under His rule and is broken over their sin.

With these characteristics of meekness in mind, what does the meek person look like? First, the meek person has a right view of himself. Again, this is a natural outcome of the first two statements that Jesus made in His sermon. A person who realizes his own spiritual bankruptcy and is broken over his sin will be meek. In reality, having a right view of yourself is to display humility.

Secondly, the meek person is happy to be a servant. He is not concerned with any position, power, prominence, prestige or profit. The world around us teaches us to be all we can and to get all we can. As a pastor, I am concerned about those who claim to be a follower of Jesus Christ, but are unwilling to serve. They want to be served rather than serve. Let's get honest here. In America, we are living in a very self-centered, selfish and proud culture that does not like to be taken out of their comfort zones. Perhaps, there are some in the Church today who are guilty of this.

Thirdly, the meek person is not easily offended. John Bunyan defined it best, "He that is down need fear no fall." The person who is offended the most is the person who thinks they had the greatest idea. But, when the idea is rejected, that person is offended. The person who is offended most is the one thinks they did the best job on a project. But, when the project is taken from them or even rejected they are offended.

Fourthly, the meek person lives in contentment. If you humble yourself, living gently and totally dependent upon God, then you will be content. Often, those who live in simplicity are those who are most content.

Let's turn our attention to a few biblical examples of individuals who were meek. Moses was a meek man. He is described as the meekest of all men who were on the earth at that time. (Numbers 12:3) He is described by God not as being a prophet who did not merely have a vision from God. Rather, God spoke to him face to face. It is even more interesting that this statement is made of Moses when complaints and accusations were being made against him. Moses was a man who had his power under control. He did not retaliate with harsh words. He turned to God. A similar incident is recorded in Numbers 16.

Another Old Testament example is Joseph. He had been sold by his jealous brothers. They lied to their father to make him think that Joseph was dead. Joseph was imprisoned. All seemed hopeless for him. Yet, God had another plan for him. He eventually found himself in the position of second in command in Egypt. If anyone had power, it was Joseph. While serving in Egypt, a moment of decision came for him. His brothers, who had started this whole thing by selling him, came to Egypt to find relief from the famine. Yet, the second most powerful man in Egypt decided to deal kindly with them. If that would have been me, I would have reminded them of what they had done to me. Then, I would have used my power as second in command to send them home and give them no grain. They could starve to death if they had done that to me! But, that is not what Joseph did. He did not abuse or misuse his power. Rather, he used it to bless the ones who had dealt so harshly with him. His power was under control. Joseph is a great example of meekness.

As you move into the New Testament you must turn to the Apostle Paul. A man who was formerly a persecutor of the church was now persecuted in the church. Paul never forgot where he came from. He never forgot what the Lord had done in his life. He dealt with people in a God honoring way. In his writings, you see a man who endured persecution with grace. He embraced what he had to go through for the sake of Christ. This is why we have the Prison Epistles. Any of us probably would have given up if we were imprisoned, Paul did not.

He used the opportunity to display meekness.

Ultimately, Jesus is the greatest example of meekness. He had all power. But, He never abused or misused it. The greatest picture of meekness in our Lord's life was in the events leading up to and on the cross. Peter described Jesus in this way, "Who, when he was reviled, reviled not again; when he suffered, he threatened not; but committed himself to him that judgeth righteously:" (1 Peter 2:25, KJV) Jesus displayed meekness as they gambled for His garments. He prayed, "Father forgive them, they do not know what they are doing." (Luke 23:34) What a picture of meekness!

The writer of Hebrews said it best when he said we are to be "looking to Jesus, the founder and perfecter of our faith, who for the joy that was set before him endured the cross, despising the shame, and is seated at the right hand of the throne of God." (Hebrews 12:2, KJV) By doing so, Jesus brought righteousness into this world so that we could experience salvation from sin. He is the one who we follow. He is the one who desires that we live holy lives. Holy lives must be characterized by meekness.

Therefore, what should meekness look like in your life as a follower of Jesus Christ? Meekness, power under control, should be displayed in every area of our lives. You should be the very best employee that has ever worked for your employer. Are you more concerned with building yourself up and moving other employees out of the way? Or, are you working for your employer in meekness and concerned about being the best employee you can be?

Meekness allows you, men, to love your wife in the way Christ loves His church. Meekness allows you, women, to willingly follow the lead of your husband. Meekness allows you, parents, to not frustrate your children. (Ephesians 5:22-6:4)

Finally, meekness is necessary in allowing the glory of God to be known among His people - the Church. They way in which we treat each other in our local church should be with humility and gentleness. This should be true among associations of churches and even among denominations. The world sees and experiences enough fighting. They need to see a people who live in and minister to each other in meekness.

# 2

## Uriah The Faithful Soldier
### 2 Samuel 11:6-8

---

**Mark Tuggle**
Centerburg Free Will Baptist

How many of you can say you are faithful?

- When I was married, when I got saved,

- Faithful = **loyal, consistent support, keeping promise**.

1Co 4:2 *Moreover it is required in stewards, that a man be found faithful.*

- This story usually is centered on David.

- Today I want to focus on Uriah and his

- Faithfulness.

- What Makes Uriah a Faithful Soldier?

I. **Faithful To Others** (Verses 9-11a)

- He was not better than others. (Lend a hand to others.)

- We should be faithful to each other and concerned.

Gal 6:2 *Bear ye one another's burdens, and so fulfil the law of Christ.*

II. **Faithful To The King and The Cause** (Vs. 11b)

- Uriah made a commitment to serving others and the King.

- We should commit to the King and surrender our lives to Him.

Mat 6:33 *But seek ye first the kingdom of God, and his righteousness; and all these things shall be added unto you.*

- In everything we do (Prayer, Service (work), attendance, etc.)

### III.   **Faithful To Death** (Vs. 14-17)

- Uriah remained faithful to Death.

- Paul remained faithful to death.

2Ti 4:6 *For I am now ready to be offered, and the time of my departure is at hand.*

2Ti 4:7 *I have fought a good fight, I have finished my course, I have kept the faith:*

2Ti 4:8 *Henceforth there is laid up for me a crown of righteousness, which the Lord, the righteous judge, shall give me at that day: and not to me only, but unto all them also that love his appearing.*

Rev 2:10 *Fear none of those things which thou shalt suffer: behold, the devil shall cast some of you into prison, that ye may be tried; and ye shall have tribulation ten days: be thou faithful unto death, and I will give thee a crown of life.*

# 3

## Committed to Christ

### 2 Timothy 1:8-12

---

**Mike Simpson**
Swauger Valley Free Will Baptists

Intro.: Paul is in prison. Yet he sends this letter of encouragement to Timothy. He begins by

1. Assuring Timothy of his continuing love and prayers and reminds him of his spiritual

2. Heritage and responsibility.

Let us focus on vs.12 *That which I have committed unto him.* Unto who? Christ.

What did he commit? Everything.

1 Peter 4:19 *Wherefore let them that suffer according to the will of God commit the keeping of their souls to him in well doing as unto a faithful Creator.*

Paul is telling Timothy *"I am committed to Christ"*. So, get committed and stay committed.

**Commitment: A promise to do or give something.** The attitude of someone who works very hard to do or support something.

Seems today people are afraid of commitment.

- They rather runaway instead of fighting thru.

- They rather throw in the towel instead of finishing the game.

- They rather live together instead of marriage.

- Some signs of lack of Commitment:

- Divorce rate is climbing.

- Few people willing to join an organization, such as, church, unions etc....

- The percentage of people who commit to attend events but fail to show is on a rise.

They say I don't want to be hemmed in. I want to

keep my options open.

Commitment means pledging yourself to a position no matter the price tag. Pledging yourself to a stance no matter the cost.

**So, let's look at commitment:**

1)    Commitment to Christ must be complete: (not lacking anything)

In Luke 9:57-62, you'll find three people who wanted to join Jesus on his journey.

a)    The Casual Follower- This man didn't understand the depth of commitment necessary to follow Jesus. This man makes a very powerful and profound promise to follow Jesus wherever he went. He wanted to be part of Jesus' work. All of these intentions are good things that might motivate some but a desire to be involved in the action is not enough. A desire to serve must also be coupled with the right reason and right motivation for serving. This man was willing to get involved but Jesus was looking for complete commitment. Vs 58 Jesus says that a person desiring to follow him must give up what others consider necessities. Jesus said, Foxes have holes and the birds of the air have nests but the Son of Man has nowhere to lay his head. The man wanted to follow Jesus but Jesus challenged him to understand the commitment to self-denial, sacrifice, service, and suffering that was necessary. The difference between involvement and commitment can be seen in a ham and egg breakfast. The chicken only has to get involved. (Give a few eggs) but the hog has to be completely committed. (He has to die) Most people settle for being involved without ever making a commitment. Being involved means that you can do what you want, when you want, and when you feel like doing it. Commitment means that you're on call 24 hrs. a day seven days a week 365 days a year. Complete commitment is what Jesus is looking for.

b)    A Caution Follower- vs 59-60 This person has misplaced priorities. Jesus says follow me but he said Lord, permit me first to go and bury my father. This man wanted to be committed on his own terms and in his own time. This man assumed commitment to family came before commitment to Christ. He said he would completely commit in the near future just not now. Vs. 60 Jesus said let the dead bury the dead. Nothing is greater than complete commitment to Christ. Jesus wanted this man to know the urgent nature of his mission. Jesus came to seek and to save that which is lost. Urgency in soul-winning. Story of Julius Caesar: When he landed on the coast of Britain with his Roman legions. He walked them up a steep mountain side and when his troops on the mountain ridge. He had all his ships burnt. So all his soldiers could see the only way off that island is thru. Full Commitment.

c)    A Careful Follower- 61-62 This one had a misdirected focus. Problem with this is he wants to follow Jesus in just a little while but not immediately. He said I will follow you Lord but first permit me to say goodbye to those at home. Let me talk it over with my family first. Knowing he would fall prey to the fervent and emotional appeal to stay home Jesus challenges him to complete commitment. Vs 62 put your hands to the plow and don't look back. This man's first commitment was to his family and not Christ. Christ must be first. Christ message is more important than anything. Commit and Don't look back. Phil.3:13 Brethren, I count not myself to have apprehended but this one thing I do forgetting those things which are behind and reaching forth unto these things which are before. Once you make your commitment don't look back. Story: A pilot of a giant airliner comes to a certain point on the runway where he has to completely commit to the air or have a great disaster. Commitment to Christ must be complete.

2)    Commitment to Christ must be Consistent: consistent means always acting or behaving the same way.

In Josh.24: He says choose you this day whom ye will serve, but for me and my house we will serve the Lord. Joshua told Israel you cannot go back and forth between God and strange gods. Commit to God and be consistent. We must be the same everyday instead of on again off again.

3)    Commitment to Christ must not be compromised: There is to be no negotiations with the devil, the world, the job, or anything else when it comes to your commitment to Christ.

**How do we commit?** Lk 9:23-25

1)    Deny yourself- your wants, desires, affections, etc....

2)    Take up your cross- your work or calling from Christ.

3)     Follow Jesus- commit to Jesus no retreat, no surrender, no regrets.

CLOSING: Commitment demands a choice. Are you committed to Christ: Completely, Consistently, Un-compromised. Or are you a casual, cautious, careful follower? Nothing but commitment will do this is what The Lord is looking for.

# 4

## Committed to the Truth
### II Timothy 1:13-18

---

**Edwin Hayes**
Ohio Free Will Baptists

**Introduction:** Those were perilous times when Paul wrote these words. The influence from false teaching was spreading and many were turning from the faith. If I have counted right, Paul mentions five men by name in this book who had fallen away and forsaken him. Men who had stood with Paul now walked away from him and his ministry. This is Paul's last known writing. When you get down to the end, your last message, you want to address the most serious issues. The trivial is cast aside and you are focused on the most important things. Paul was handing the mantle of his ministry over to his young son in the faith, Timothy.

He knew that he would soon be gone and wouldn't be able to personally influence Timothy and the church. So what would he say? What would you say at a time like this? Paul wanted the ministry to continue through Timothy. It is no accident that in this book that Paul brings up to Timothy his commitment to Christ. We must know Him, believe Him, trust Him, not be ashamed of Him and confidently rest in Him. He is the reason we are all here tonight.

Then he turns to the second commitment that Timothy would need and that is a commitment to the truth. *"Hold fast the form of sound words, which thou hast heard of me..."* II Tim. 1:13. He was to be committed to the truth. There are three things about the truth: The truth *never changes*, the *truth is what corresponds to reality* and the truth *not what we want it to be, but what it is.* The truth would be the anchor that would hold Timothy's faith and soul, even in the most difficult times.

Our society's greatest problem is not gay marriage, abortion or even the breakdown of the family. These are all just symptoms of the greater problem of the falling away from the commitment to God's truth!

This evening I would like to see what will keep us in these perilous times in which we live-it was the same as in Timothy's day. We must be committed to these sound words that we have heard.

**The Exhortation (vs. 13)**

Timothy was to be committed to those words *"Hold fast..."*. The spirit of desertion had captured even those who walked with Paul. He gave the warning in chapter 3:13-17 of how the last days would look. There would be perilous times when men would be *lovers of themselves, covetous, boasters, proud, blasphemers, disobedient to parents, unthankful, unholy, without natural affection, trucebreakers, false accusers, incontinent, fierce, despisers of those that are good, traitors, heady, high-minded, lovers of pleasures more than lovers of God;...*

Paul also gave the encouragement and charge of chapter 4:2 to *"Preach the word;..."*. He was to guard the truth. He was to keep the deposit given to him. He was not to allow the truth to be corrupted through *distortion, dilution, deletion* and *addition.* You see the truth doesn't need to be changed or updated but simply proclaimed. False teaching is always a constant threat to the truth!

We should be committed to this words as well. In the past we in America have enjoyed many great supports for truth. There was a time when the *culture* supported the truth. There was a time when the *society* supported the truth. There was a time when the *schools* supported the truth. There was a time when the *courts* supported the truth. There was a time when the *government* supported the truth. There was a time when most *churches* and *denominations* supported the truth. This has served America well. We have enjoyed a Biblical world view and the blessings that came with it. Most of us have grown up with this.

In the present, America has cast off belief in Christ

and absolute truth. Gradually most of these supports are now gone. There is one lone voice who is still committed to the truth. The church seems to be alone in proclaiming truth, much like Jeremiah giving his unpopular but truthful message to Jerusalem! We are still proclaiming there is an absolute truth, God has created man and holds him accountable, men are sinners, there is only one Savior and there is only one way to heaven.

Have you noticed how proclaiming truth makes people angry? With no Biblical worldview, they have gone the way of Romans 1. (This is not the first time this has happened!) They say there is no special creation and with accepting evolution they have no accountability to God. To them man is simply an animal and not made in the image of God.

The results of this thinking has brought us all these modern day movements: abortion, homosexuality, gay marriage, the right to die, the move to legalize drugs, seeing no value in the church, in fact a growing hostility toward the church. Also we see the movement to attack the Bible and ultimately God Himself is under attack. These all "make sense" to the world!

What will keep us in the evil day when men's ideas and philosophies are swirling around? The best defense against apostasy is to be committed to the truth. Keeping the word in faith and love. This Bible has kept us, showed us God's love, His salvation, how to live in this present world and to one day step on heaven's shore! No other book does this! What does the world offer that compares to this? Thank the Lord for His eternal truth that will stand when this world is gone!

**The Energy (vs. 14)**

It is wonderful to know that we are not alone in this battle. Imagine if we were all alone with all the enemies that stand against us? We are kept by the Holy Spirit who dwells in us. He will keep the good thing (deposit) He has entrusted us with a most valuable gift. He will give us the energy and power to withstand the onslaughts of this evil day.

At the close of WW II, two pictures appeared in a magazine showing a soldier in conflict with a tank. The first showed a huge tank bearing down on a tiny soldier, about to crush him. The picture was proportioned to show the odds involved when a footsoldier with a rifle faced a tank. The next picture showed what happened to that soldier's odds with a bazooka, or rocket launcher in his hands. This time the tank appeared to be shrunken in size and the soldier at least equal in size, if not a little bigger. *Illustrations for Biblical Preaching, Michael P. Green* Illustration 661. On our own we would be like that tiny soldier before that tank, but with the Holy Spirit our odds change greatly!

There are three qualifiers for the Holy Spirit to be our energy in this fight. 1. If we submit to His leadership. 2. If we cultivate a true intimate daily relationship and walk with the Lord! 3. If we understand that it does not matter what we do for the Lord in public if we have not been with Him in private!

A.C. Dixon said, "When we rely on organization, we get what organization can do. When we rely upon education, we get what education can do. When we rely upon eloquence, we get what eloquence can do. When we rely on the Holy Spirit, we get what God can do. *Knight's Treasury of Illustrations*

### The Examples (vs. 15-18)

In verse 15 we see the bad examples of those who deserted Paul-(all those in Asia). Singled out were Phygellus and Hermogenes who had abandoned Paul! Two more, Philetus and Hymenaeus were mentioned in chapter 2:16-18, and Demas was pointed out in chapter 4:10. I would sure hate to have my name in the Bible for this reason! These are people who had received Christ, believed the truth, knew Paul and have evidently ministered for the Lord and then deserted Paul!

We have all seen people that loved the Lord and served the Lord but they are not today! Why would they do this? Could it have been the pressure of ministry? Could it be that they just grew tired of the fight? Could it have been not wanting to be considered "odd" to the world? For Demas we know the reason-he loved the world! I wonder what all these people would say to us now? These are not the examples we should follow.

In verses 16-18 we see the good example of Onesiphorus who was not ashamed, not afraid, sought Paul out, ministered to him. He had the same temptations as the others, but he remained faithful! Onesiphorus lets us know it is not impossible to stay committed even in the most difficult circumstances.

There is a verse in the Bible that sometimes I don't like very much. It is found in Proverbs 24:10 *"If thou faint in the day of adversity, thy strength is small."* The reason that I sometimes do not like the verse is that it doesn't allow me to excuse myself or blame others for my own failures! According to this verse, if I fail it is because I didn't have the strength myself. I must bear the blame!

Tonight we must not fail! We have a truth that is worth fighting for, worth keeping holding onto, worth dying for, worth anticipating a reward for. In the 1976 Summer Olympics, Shu Fujimoto competed in team gymnastics competition for Japan. In a quest for the gold medal Fujimoto suffered a broken right knee in the floor exercise. But his injury did not stop him, for during the next week he competed in his strongest event, the rings. His routine was excellent, but he astounded everyone by squarely dismounting with a triple somersault twist on a broken right knee. When asked concerning his feat, he said, "Yes, the pain shot through me like a knife. It bought rears to my eyes. But now I have a gold medal and the pain is gone. *Illustrations for Biblical Preaching, Michael P. Green*

**Conclusion:** As Paul reminded Timothy that he needed to hold fast to these sound words, we need the same exhortation. These words will hold us in place while this nation literally destroys itself with its foolish philosophy. Let us remember that we are not alone in this battle-God has supplied the energy we need. We have the examples before us. Let's recommit ourselves to the truth, basing our lives, our marriages, our families, our churches, our ministries and our denomination on it.

# 5

## Committed to Others
### 2 Timothy 2.1-7

---

### Mike Gladson
Canaan Free Will Baptists

What will the people who knew you best say about you when you're gone? We all know that casual acquaintances can say what they want, and it doesn't really matter because they never really knew us.

But you can't fool your children or your spouse or parents or your closest friends. *They know the truth because they've lived with you so long and seen you in so many different circumstances.* What will they say about you as they walk back to their cars while your casket is being lowered into the ground? How will you be remembered?

*For the Apostle Paul, that was no idle question*. When he wrote II Timothy, he was in prison, in chains, in Rome, under a sentence of imminent death. His days were numbered. He didn't have five years left and he probably didn't have five months to get his act together. The grains of sand had nearly all slipped from the hourglass. Death by beheading was not far away. Paul knew he would never get out of prison alive. That's why he said, "I have finished my course." For him the race of life was almost over.

<u>**Only one thing was left to do**</u>: Send a message to his young protégé, Timothy, and give him a final word of encouragement. Then he could face his death with grace and courage.

Paul was a committed man.

He was committed to the gospel but also committed to others. He was interested in the spiritual welfare of others. He was interested that the gospel continued even after his death.

As Paul faced the close of his ministry he knew the importance of faithfulness on the part of the next generation.

- Paul knew the hardships and the persecution they would face.
- He knew false doctrine and the watering down of truth would be a serious problem for the church.

If you know you're about to die, you don't waste time and you don't waste words. You get right to the point. Paul gives Timothy pieces of advice:

## AS A SON, BE STRENTHENED BY GOD'S GRACE – 2.1

Paul has shared with Timothy his disappointment over the growing apostasy that was spreading through Asia. As he turns to Timothy he is emphatic that he wants Timothy of all people to be among those who are not ashamed of the gospel even in the face of persecution.

Difficult circumstances, our own weaknesses and fears, and the negative attitudes or unfaithfulness of others should not determine our course of life.

This is our calling, our challenge; this is our mission from God. Be strong in the Lord. Stand strong in the grace of Jesus Christ.

- When times are tough, be strong.
- When you feel like giving up, be strong.

To be strong speaks of moral courage in the face of unrelenting opposition.

***To be strong in grace means that you don't rely on yourself when times are tough, you rely on the Lord alone.***

That's the moral qualification.

***"be strong"*** means to strengthen yourself. It is a

directive to be obeyed in a continuous way. This can be paraphrased this way:

## KEEP ON BEING EMPOWERED OR KEEP IN TOUCH WITH THE POWER (A.T. Robertson)

Spiritual weakness plagues all of us. Spiritual weakness can come from fatigue, frustration, and seemingly insurmountable obstacles in the Lord's work.

Timothy was facing a time of weakness:

- He may have been questioning his calling or his gifts
- or the sufficiency of God's provisions.

He was mired in difficulties and was sinking fast! Whatever he was facing, Paul realized that his son in the faith need to *"stir up the gift of God which is in thee.." 2 Tim. 1.6.*

**Illus:** After Moses died, Joshua faced insurmountable obstacles in the Lords work. The Lord encouraged Joshua by saying Joshua 1.9

**Jos. 1.9** Have not I commanded thee? Be strong and of a good courage; be not afraid, neither be thou dismayed: for the Lord thy God *is* with thee whithersoever thou goest.

Whatever we do, keep in touch with the power!

## AS A TEACHER/MENTOR, PASS DOWN TRUTH TO OTHERS – 2.2

Paul had a specific purpose in mind for Timothy's increasing strength. Paul is preparing Timothy for his departure so must Timothy prepare others to take his place one day who in turn prepares others. And the chain continues...

The gospel is to be passed down from generation to generation. Jesus Himself is the master teacher. He spent his three years of public ministry with 12 men, the apostles, and taught them. They taught others who taught others. This has continued throughout the church age.

2:2. Traveling with Paul, Timothy had heard the apostle address scores of diverse audiences. Among all those groups the essence of Paul's message had not changed. It was the same body of truth Paul had taught Timothy personally.

Paul had a deep concern for the truth of the gospel in Ephesus. He would later ask Timothy to leave Ephesus and join him in Rome (4:9, 21). Paul wanted Timothy to pass gospel truths to reliable men. These trustworthy men could keep the home front secure against heresy. Note the close relationship between the task of this verse and the imperatives of 1:13–14.

The *"things"* Timothy was to pass down were the foundational truths of the gospel

There is always an inclination for some to add to or take away from the truth that has been entrusted to them.  Paul did not do this (2 Cor. 2.17, 4.2)

Much of the content of first and second Tim.
Is to encourage Timothy to get to know the truth.  Note 2 Tim. 1.13, 2.15, 3.1,14

It is TRUTH Paul is concerned with not Tradition

It is SUBSTANCE Paul is concerned with not Style

How often truth is lost in style and tradition!

Paul was concerned that the truth of the gospel would be transmitted from one generation of Christians to another

**Illus:** When I was in middle school I ran track.  One of the races was the mile relay.  It was important that all four of us prepare and learn what it meant to pass the baton to each other.  Dropping the baton meant disqualification.  So we practiced proper handoffs so that the race would be won.

It seems that the Americans in the Olympic Games have become experts in dropping the baton.  At the Beijing Olympics, the United States men's and women's 4x100-meter relay teams dropped batons — and heard the pings of them hitting the track — during a disastrous performance.

Four years earlier in Athens, shoddy baton passing by the American men had allowed a British relay team to pull off an upset, while the United States women were disqualified after a botched exchange.

Nobody wants the embarrassment of being the one who drops the baton or who botches the exchange. The purpose of the race is that the baton crosses the finish line through one person passing it to another person who passes it to another person, etc.

**APPLY:** We have been entrusted with the gospel. We must make sure that the gospel truth is passed down from one generation to another and that we don't "drop the baton" in the process.

## AS A SOLDIER, HAVE A SINGLENESS OF PURPOSE TO SERVE THE LORD – 2.3-4

Paul used military imagery in many of his letters. He understood that Christian living involved warfare

Paul tells Timothy to:

### 1.    Endure hardships

"Endure hardness" - similar to 1.8.  Maybe Timothy was a bit reluctant to face hardship.  All of us are to some degree.  Maybe he did not maintain courage in the face of challenges.  Again, all of us are like that.

To endure hardness means to suffer together with someone.  Timothy was to join the ranks of those who bear suffering.

Soldiers on active duty expect hardship. Battling the enemy on the front lines, the soldier lives in harsh conditions—damp weather, poor food, uncomfortable sleep, dirt and filth, inadequate shelter, and exhaustion.

The further someone retreats from the front lines, however, the more frequent and trivial become the complaints. Those involved in the struggles of survival and the exhaustion of combat rarely complain about the food—they are simply happy to eat.

In the same way, Christians who determine to live holy, obedient lives before God place themselves on the front lines of spiritual warfare.

They encounter:
- Counter attacks of Satan,
- Suffer scorn and rejection,
- And often deny themselves many comforts.

### 2.    Be separate from the world

The term, "entangleth himself" speaks of the importance of separation from the world.  The phrase means to weave be caught up and enmeshed in them.

Many have entangled themselves like Demas in 4.10.

### 3.    Have a singleness of purpose

Paul's appeal shows the importance of developing an ability to distinguish between doing good things and doing the best things. Servants of Christ are not merely to be well-rounded dabblers in all types of trivial pursuits.

They are tough-minded devotees of Christ who constantly choose the right priorities from a list of potential selections. Paul prohibited the loss of single-mindedness and the longing for an easy life.

**Note:** Why endure hardness? Why should there be separation from the world? Why have a singleness of purpose? The reason for all this: 'that he may please him." The ambition of the Christian soldier must be that of pleasing the Lord.

Paul wanted the approval of the Lord 2.1, 2.15, 2.21, 4.8

## AS AN ATHLETE, PLAY BY GOD'S RULES – 2.5

Paul turned next to athletic competition for his illustration, focusing on the commitment that proceeds from honest and legitimate faith. Sports were probably as popular during the days of the Roman Empire as they are now.

Each game or contest has particular rules that help define the sport and describe proper conduct and etiquette; no athlete makes up the rules he goes along. If someone breaks these rules or ignores them, the officials disqualify him.

Christian living also requires adherence to certain rules regarding purity, doctrinal orthodoxy, faith, and love. Those who abide by the truth of God's Word will receive their reward on the Day of Judgment. Those who try to claim the prize without a commitment to faithful obedience will be disqualified.

## AS A FARMER, WORK WITH AN EYE ON THE FUTURE – 2.6

The picture of the farmer is in contrast to glamour and excitement of being in a race with it's onlookers and crowing ceremony to the patient work the farmer does that is hard and often goes unnoticed.

How often a farmer grows weary and exhausted. But we know that the harvest belongs to him that labors in the field.

Paul is saying to his young preacher: Don't by relaxing the labor lose that right!

By keeping an eye on the future, the farmer's hard work keeps him laboring during the growing season. If he becomes negligent to his attention to detail, he will never see the harvest!!

**APPLY:** God has called each of us to ministry. It's a long way between the enthusiastic beginning and our anticipated glory in seeing Jesus. There is a lot of hard work in between.

Everyone committed to the life of faith will deal with difficult circumstances, issues of temptation, spiritual struggles, adverse opinions of others, misunderstandings, exhaustion etc.

Paul was committed to others, especially seen in Timothy.

**Conclusion:** With all of this in mind Paul instructs Timothy in *2.7 "consider what I say..."*

Paul desired his protégé understand fully and ponder in his mind these thoughts.  Look at your life and ask yourself:

- Am I a strong Christian?
- Am I devoted to guarding and teaching God's Word?

- Do I keep a distance between myself and the affairs of the world?

- Am I playing by the rules?

- Am I willing to work when no one notices me and praises me so that I will enjoy the harvest?

We are promised if we can say yes to these questions that the *"Lord will give understanding in all things" v.7*

We will have wisdom and insight through all the challenges to victory!

# 6

## Devotion
### Colossians 3:23, 24

---

**John Wallace**
Beatty Free Will Baptist

**HEARTILY**: Out of one's soul, from the core of one's being.

**PASSION**: Intense driving from within. God is the source of our passion. It is discovered when we find God's gift within us.

#1. **Passions pursues**. Passion is David loving God with his whole heart, obeying the word with his whole heart, praying with his whole heart.

#2. **Passion pledges**. David states that he will praise God and reject all other gods.

#3.    **Passion confronts.**    Passion is Elijah challenging the Baal prophets and calling fire down from God.

#4.    **Passion produces.** Passion is Nehemiah building the wall of Jerusalem in 52 days against all odds.

#5.    **Passion persists.** Passion is Jeremiah not quitting the ministry in spite of discouragement, the fire in his bones would not let him quit.

#6.    **Passion prays.** Passion is Daniel praying in spite of threats against his life because prayer was the heartbeat of his life.

#7.    **Passion moves.** Passion is Peter jumping into the water walking to Jesus in spite of the "impossibility" of it.

#8.    Passion motivates. Passion is the Apostle Paul turning the zeal of his past into a fire for the cause of Christ.

# 7

## Does The Devil Know Your Name

### Acts 19:11-15

---

**Mark Tuggle**
Centerburg Free Will Baptist

- The devil would like nothing more than to kill you.
- Physically, mentally, emotionally, and spiritually.
- He is a thief.
- .

John 10:10 *The thief cometh not, but for to steal, and to kill, and to destroy: I am come that they might have life, and that they might have it more abundantly.*

Joh 10:11 I am the good shepherd: the good shepherd giveth his life for the sheep.

---

1Pe 5:8 *Be sober, be vigilant; because your adversary the devil, as a roaring lion, walketh about, seeking whom he may devour:*

- How did the evil spirit know Paul?
- How do you know if the devil knows your name?

### I.  You Believe in Christ

Paul Believed. (Everything he touched.) Paul Preached.

Rom 1:16 *For I am not ashamed of the gospel of Christ: for it is the power of God unto salvation to everyone that believeth; to the Jew first, and also to the Greek.*

**Do you know who else believes?**

Jas 2:19 *Thou believest that there is one God; thou doest well: the devils also believe, and tremble.*

**The devil will know your name if you believe.**

Rom 10:9 *That if thou shalt confess with thy mouth the Lord Jesus, and shalt believe in thine heart that God hath raised him from the dead, thou shalt be saved.*

### II. You Confess Christ

- The devil knew Paul confessed Christ.
- Paul shared his conversion to others.

1Co 2:2 *For I determined not to know anything among you, save Jesus Christ, and him crucified.*

Rom 10:10 *For with the heart man believeth unto righteousness; and with the mouth confession is made unto salvation.*

### III.    You Show Christ
- The evil spirit knew Paul showed Christ.
- When you have a life changing experience with Christ the devil knows

2Co 5:15 *And that he died for all, that they which live should not henceforth live unto themselves, but unto him which died for them, and rose again.*

### Does the devil know your name?
- Do you believe in Christ?
- Do you Confess Christ?
- Do you Show Christ?

# 8

## Be A Generational Visionary

---

### Mike Mounts
Harrison Free Will Baptist

**What is a Generational Visionary?** It is a person whose vision for their children, grandchildren, and great grandchildren is for them to live a victorious Christian life that will bring glory to God and a benefit to the people around them. It also involves taking the necessary actions to best insure that the generational vision is faithfully passed on to the following generations. It means trusting God to do His marvelous redeeming work while doing all you can to point those following you in the direction of an active, vibrant relationship with Jesus Christ. Finally, it means being the consummate example of a true born-again Christian and a generational visionary.

**Who was a generational visionary?** There are many people in the Bible that fill this role. There are two that exemplify in word and deed what a generational visionary looks like.

### Jonadab, the Rechabite (around 842 BC)
**See II Kings 10:15, Jeremiah 35:1-10, and Nehemiah 3:14**

Jonadab descended from Jethro, the father-in-law of Moses. He was not a Jew, but his family believed in and worshipped the God of Abraham, Isaac, and Jacob. When he saw the moral decline in the nation of Israel, he realized that Israel would decay to the point that they would be conquered by a strong, heathen nation. He commanded his children and grandchildren to live a nomadic life and refrain from (1) drinking wine, (2) living in houses, (3) sowing seed, and (4) planting vineyards. He wanted them to be mobile so that they could escape when Israel was conquered.

We find this out from his descendants about 250 years after his death, eight generations later, who were still obeying his commands. He had such a profound effect on his children and grandchildren that they perpetuated his commands. They survived the capture of Israel by the Assyrians, but also the capture of Judah by the Babylonians. We read of a Rechabite working on the rebuilding of the wall around Jerusalem in the time of Nehemiah, around 400 years after Jonadab lived. God promised the family of Jonadab that there would never be a time when a descendant of Jonadab would not be serving God.

### Josiah, King of Judah (640 – 609 BC)
### See II Kings, chapters 22- 24.

Josiah became the king of Judah at the age of eight and died at the age of 40. He became king when Judah was in serious moral decline having forsaken the worship of the one true God for worship of the idol Baal. Yet, he was a righteous king who did all he could to step the destructive tide. He spearheaded significant repairs to the Solomon's Temple in Jerusalem. While doing those repairs, the high priest "found" the book of the law and brought it to Josiah to. When Josiah realized what the law said, he was very interested in what it meant for the backsliding Jews of his day. Through a prophetess God told Josiah that it meant that He was going to judge Judah and bring punishment upon them, but that Josiah would not see it in his lifetime.

Josiah could have reacted to the prophecy from God the same way his great grandfather, Hezekiah, had reacted when given the same prophecy, who simply responded that it was a good thing that God's judgment did not come in his lifetime. (See II Kings 20:16-19). Conversely, Josiah went to work and led the people of Jerusalem in a time of repentance and a commitment to follow the ways of God. Regardless of what was coming, he wanted to lead as many young people as possible in getting right with God. Only a few years after Josiah's death, King Nebuchadnezzar of Babylon conquered Judah and took thousands of young people from Judah to Babylon. Included in that group were Daniel and the three Hebrew children, who faithfully lived for the Lord God Jehovah all their lives while they served four heathen kings. Undoubtedly these four stalwarts of the faith were influenced by the work and words of Josiah.

**Will you be a Generational Visionary?** You can have such a close, vibrant relationship with your children and grandchildren and maybe even your great grandchildren that they will naturally follow your example and your righteous living and will themselves pass that on to their descendants. There are a few critical steps that you can take to insure that this progression of faithful Christian descendants continues even after you die.

1.   Write your children and grandchildren letters.
2.   Ask bonding questions of them.
3.   Teach them about the pavilions of protection that God provides them.

Details of these steps are listed on the next page. After you read through these steps you may have a number of reasons for why this won't work for you. You may have a strained relationship with some of your children and grandchildren. There may be painful past episodes in these relationships. Write the letters anyway. The worst that can happen is that the person will come back to you in anger because of past events. This then becomes an opportunity to open up much-needed communication. Those past issues need to be resolved through confession, asking forgiveness, and giving forgiveness. Even though difficult, these kinds of conversations will be critical in perpetuating a continued relationship that will insure the ongoing process of being a generational visionary.

**Take The Challenge,
Take The Opportunity,
Take The Responsibility**

**Ten Letters To Write Your Children And Grandchildren**

1. You are a gift from God.
2. You are dearly loved.
3. You are designed for great works.
4. You have marks of ownership.
5. You have a significant name.
6. You have birth-order tendencies.
7. You have a motivational gift.
(Proclaimer, Server, Teacher, Exhorter,
Giver, Organizer, Mercy Shower)
8. You have a unique family heritage.
9. You have three powerful enemies.
(Anger, Greed, Lust)
10. You have seven important decisions.
    a. Wanting God's best
    b. Dedicate your body to God
    c. Seek the Lord
    d. Be a "Giver", not a "Taker"
    e. Maintain a clear conscience
    f. Honor your parents and grandparents
    g. Righteously fulfill seven basic needs.
       i. To know God
       ii. To be special to those you admire
       iii. To share your heart
       iv. To be understood
       v. To do great works
       vi. To have our work last after we die
       vii. To receive recognition for Achievements

## FIFTEEN BONDING QUESTIONS TO ASK YOUR CHILDREN AND GRANDCHILDREN

1.  Who is your best friend?
2.  What do you want to do in your life?
3.  What fears do you experience?
4.  What books have influenced you the most?
5.  What things in our family discourage you?
6.  Which of these things is the most pressing issue to you?
7.  What changes do you want to see in me?
8.  What do you enjoy doing most in your free time?
9.  What hurts have you experienced from people?
10. What thing in your past would you like to change?
11. If you could talk to God face to face, what would you ask?
12. What person do you respect the most?
13. How would you describe your relationship with God?
14. Has God ever worked supernaturally in your life?
15. Is there anything you are afraid to talk to me about?

## TEACH THEM GOD'S PAVILIONS OF PROTECTION

1.  The pavilion of the power of Christ (over our weaknesses) – II Corinthians 12:7-10.
2.  The pavilion of patience – Romans 5:3-5, Hebrews 10:36
3.  The pavilion of faith – Ephesians 6:16, I Peter 5:8, II Timothy 1:7
4.  The pavilion of a covenant – Galatians 3:8-9,

Romans 8:1-3
    5.   Symbolic pictures of protection
        a.   The protective covering of the Ark – Matthew 24:37-39, I Peter 3:20-21
        b.   The protective covering of a house – Joshua 2:19
        c.   The protective covering of the cloud – Psalm 105:37-45
        d.   The protective covering of God's Tabernacle – Psalm 27:4-5
        e.   The protective covering of God's "Wings" – Psalm 17:8, 36:7, 91:4
        f.   The protective covering of a woman's hair – Ephesians 5:25, I Corinthians 11:10, 15

This is just a basic outline. Much more detail is needed to implement these steps effectively. Two soft-bound books that can further help you develop these steps are: **A Father's Treasures** and **Pavilions of Protection**, both from the

**FIVE PERSPECTIVES IN ASKING THESE 15 BONDING QUESTIONS**
    A.   Demonstrate a hearing (understanding) heart.
    B.   Honor and praise each answer.
    C.   Don't correct and counsel during this time.
    D.   Take notes for prayer and future projects.
    E.   Be patient for secret failures.
    F.   Include God in your discussions.

# 9

## Show Me The Body
### Mark 16:1-5

---

### Mike Mounts
Harrison Free Will Baptist

This sermon is an exegetical look at the burial and resurrection of Christ, as recorded in the last chapter of the Gospel of Mark. We will explore the visit to the tomb of the women disciples, the anointing of Christ, the sealed tomb, and the women's response to the man in white. This message was first preached at Canaan Land Free Will Baptist Church on April 5, 2015.

In verse one we find that the women Disciples of Christ came to the tomb with the purpose of anointing the body of Jesus with sweet spices that they had bought for that purpose. The intention of the women was to finish the work of the burial that had begun just before evening on the day that Christ was crucified. The Bible clearly states that it was late in the day when Joseph of Arimathaea requested the Savior's body for burial. Pilate first verified that Jesus was indeed dead so soon as crucifixion deaths  had been known to last up to three days before the victim was confirmed as lifeless. Each day on the Jewish calendar starts in the evening, and can be seen as a response to the schedule that God foreordained during the creation event (in Genesis chapter 1: the evening and the morning were the  first day; the evening and the morning were the second day; and so on). So each day began in the evening, at sunset, rather than at midnight as we traditionally hold today in the United States. The next day (starting at sunset on the day of crucifixion) was the Sabbath, so Joseph and the other disciples who helped in the burial process did not have much time to prepare Jesus' body for burial. It is noteworthy that the Gospel of John records that Nicodemus brought a hundred pounds of spices to use in wrapping the body of Jesus in linen grave-cloths. The linen would-be wound together with a mixture of myrrh, aloe, and cassia spices that would create a gum-like coating over the linen. What is significant is that Nicodemus brought a hundred pounds of these spices...normally only fifty pounds was used in *royal* burial ceremonies. Kings would be buried with fifty pounds, but bless God... Nicodemus must have recognized that here would lay one greater than the kings of the earth; here would lay the King of Kings, and Lord of Lords! It is thought that the majority of the spices would be placed in the bottom of the  linen wrappings, underneath the body. In the other gospels, it is mentioned that the disciples saw the grave-cloths "folded together" - think about this: if I wrap my hand in a cloth, and then remove my hand, what happens to the cloth? It folds together, because what supported it from the inside is no longer there. Thus, the accounts of the grave-cloths witnessed as folded together is consistent with the supernatural resurrection of Christ. This flies in the face of the logically misguided thought that Jesus was simply incoherent, and then woke up in the tomb, which would imply that he removed the grave- cloths a piece at a time.

So the women came to anoint the body of Jesus, but Jesus was already anointed, as it is written: "Thou lovest righteousness, and hatest wickedness: therefore God, thy God, hath anointed thee with the oil of gladness above thy fellows. All thy garments smell of myrrh, and aloes, and cassia, out of the ivory palaces, whereby they have made thee glad." (Ps. 45:7-8; as a side note - this psalm is referencing a bridegroom's traditional preparation for his wedding; how much more was Jesus, the Bridegroom of the church, preparing for His...!).

"The Spirit of the Lord God is upon me; because the Lord hath anointed me to preach good tidings unto the meek; he hath sent me to bind up the brokenhearted, to proclaim liberty to the captives, and the opening of the prison to them that are bound;" (Is. 61:1)

And again: "That word, I say, ye know, which was published throughout all Judea, and began from Galilee, after the baptism which John preached; How God anointed Jesus of Nazareth with the Holy Ghost and with power: who went about doing good, and healing all that were oppressed of the devil; for God was with him." (Acts 10:37-38)

The women came to the tomb at the rising of the sun in verse two, but the Son had already risen! How comforting it is to know that when you woke up this morning, God was already sitting on His throne. When you poured your first cup of coffee, He was already attentive to your needs. For those of you who are saved - when you got dressed for church, He had already clothed you in His righteousness; and  when you reached out to Him in prayer, He was already prepared to answer!

The women asked, in verse three, "Who shall roll us away the stone from the door of the sepulchre?" There was a stone that guarded the entrance of the tomb, that was sealed by Roman counsel, and that stood in the way of their ministry to the body of Christ. The seal that was placed on the stone was marked by Roman authority, so before these women could even consider finding someone physically strong enough to move the stone out of their way, they would first need to find someone who would be willing to plead their cause before Roman officials (in essence- with the request for Rome to consider reversing their decision to place the seal there in the first place). This Roman seal was likely a rope affixed to the tomb, and had a wax insignia that bore the inscription of Rome. So while skeptics will say that the women likely came to the wrong tomb and found it empty, it would have been easy enough for the women to just look at the tomb and see where the seal was originally placed. How many other tombs would have been through the process of being sealed by Rome during this time? The Roman process for sealing something required the assigned Roman authority figure to verify the contents of that which was to be sealed. There was no mistake that this was the tomb of Jesus. Also worth noting is that unauthorized tampering or removal of a Roman seal was punishable by death. What is it in our lives that keeps *us* from ministering to the body of Christ? Satan will often (if we let him) place a stumbling block in front of where God wants us to minister, that is not only too heavy of a burden for us to move, but sealed with authority that is above ours, and guarded by those that standby. You cannot minister to the body of Christ with sin in your life. The sin has to be completely removed before you will ever be effective in your ministry for Him. Thank God for Jesus - who pleads our case before God, and asks for a reversal of the decision which is pronounced against us! God, Himself, rolled the stone away, broke the seal, and drove the guards away with an earthquake - at just the right time. God not only has the power to remove sin in our lives, and that which keeps us from ministering for Him, but He has the authority to do so. There is no seal that can be placed on the sin in your life that God does not have the authority, or the willingness, to remove. The women started out for the tomb early in the morning, fully knowing that they did not have what it took to get into where they had last seen Christ - but they came anyway, and God intervened. Maybe you know that there are things in your life that are keeping you from the ministry; that are keeping you from being effective for Christ; that stand in between you and the body of Christ... maybe you should do what the women did - come anyway. Make your way down to an altar of prayer, and maybe just as these women - where you last saw the body of Christ.

The women really had no reason to be scared, but this surprise in the way God was working resulted in their fear. The last words of verse five state "...they were affrighted". How many times have we been scared of doing God's will, because of how He is working to make it happen? Just as there was an earthquake that shook the ground where these women stood, we shouldn't be surprised if when we come to God, that He shakes the very ground on which we stand. He may shake the very foundations that your life is built upon - your family, your job, even your church life. But He has a purpose- and that purpose is in our best interest. For He has said "I know the thoughts that I think toward you... thoughts of peace, and not of evil, to give you an expected end." (Jer. 29:11)That expected end includes a resurrection:

"Blessed and holy is he that hath part in the first resurrection: on such the second death hath no power, but they shall be priests of God and of Christ, and shall reign with him a thousand years." (Rev. 20:6)

# 10

## Wave Petunias

---

### Mike Mounts
Harrison Free Will Baptist

Most of you already know how much I enjoy working in the yard—planting flowers, landscaping, and yes, even mowing the grass. Over the past couple weeks Sandy and I have really worked hard, as we planted flowers around the house and laid some landscape brick. We also planted a few tomato plants. But when it comes to landscaping, I mentioned to Sandy that I might be slow, but I'm cheap.

A few years ago I discovered a fairly new petunia called a wave petunia. Unlike the old fashioned petunia, the wave petunia spreads. In fact, they spread so well you have to keep them trimmed. They'll take over a flower bed!

After planting them, I wanted to see if it was wise to "deadhead" (prune by removing old blooms) them while they were still fairly young plants. So I got on the internet and looked up "deadheading" wave petunias. While looking, I found the following illustration from *Proven Winners* website.

"In the grand scheme of things flowers are meant *to ensure survival of the species.* All of the various blooms that nature developed (not plant breeders) are an attempt *to ensure that seeds are produced and the next generation of plants develops.*"(Italics added)

Although I read the next line, I almost missed its spiritual relevance:

"In some cases, once seed has been produced thus ensuring the survival of the species, the plant will stop blooming since there is no reason to put energy into blooming any longer." [Wow!]

In one sense, the flower exists in order to produce a new generation of flowers, so that the flower may perpetuate after its own kind. It doesn't merely exist for itself—it exists for future generations.

It seems that we've had a bumper crop of dandelions this year. Did you know that there are 60-100 seeds on the head of a dandelion? There's a house on the way to Lucasville with a huge maple tree in the front yard. It's loaded with seeds. You know, those little helicopters that blow in the wind? Those little fellows are bottom heavy so when they fall to the ground, the seed is pointed downward and driven into the soil by gravity and the rain. Absolutely amazing!

At the house where I grew up, we had one huge maple tree in the front yard. (As a boy, I even climbed clear to the top of it a couple times). At least two maple trees came up voluntarily in the side yard from its seeds. In fact, after Sandy I were married and moved into a mobile home park outside of Springfield, I dug up one of the trees and transplanted it in our front yard. If that tree's still alive, guess what it's still doing? It's producing more seeds in order to produce more trees!

Consider tomatoes. Tomatoes are grown, not merely for food, but also for seeds. The seeds are planted *to produce the next generation of tomatoes and to ensure the survival of the species.* What about corn? Yes, we grow corn to eat, but it is must also be grown for seed *to produce the next generation of corn and to ensure the survival of the species.* We do the same thing with beans and potatoes. I'm sure we've all heard of *seed* potatoes.

God gave us these things for food. However, He also gave us seeds from them in order to sow or plant—to perpetuate the seed *and* the food. Right? What would happen if we just ate all the produce that we grow? What would happen if there were no more seeds? What would happen if there were no more sowing, planting, gardening, or farming?

What would happen if there was a halt to the reproduction of beef cattle, milk cows, or chickens? What would preachers do without fried chicken?

Still God intended for each plant and animal to reproduce after its kind (Gen. 1). It's innate within each species to reproduce after its own kind. **Each species doesn't merely exist for itself—it exists for future generations**. What happens to a family name when there is no reproduction?

God blessed Adam and Eve and said to them, "Be fruitful and multiply; fill the earth and subdue it." After the flood, God spoke similar words to Noah and his sons. It wasn't just about them and their generation—it was about future generations. In fact, from the line of Shem came Abraham, Isaac, Jacob, Judah, Boaz, Jesse, David, and ultimately Jesus! It wasn't merely about one generation; it was about the redemption of the world!

Note the words of Jesus and how He illustrates His death:

Most assuredly, I say to you, unless a grain of wheat falls into the ground and dies [germination], it remains alone; but if it dies, it produces much grain [a great harvest of souls!]. (John. 12:24)

Consider the words of Jesus from John 15:1-8, 16 (italics added for emphasis):

"I am the true vine, and My Father is the vinedresser. Every branch in Me that does not bear fruit He takes away; and every *branch* that bears fruit He prunes, *that it may bear more fruit*. You are already clean because of the word which I have spoken to you. Abide in Me, and I in you. As the branch cannot bear fruit of itself, unless it abides in the vine, neither can you, unless you abide in Me. I am the vine, you *are* the branches. He who abides in Me, and I in him, *bears much fruit*; for without Me you can do nothing. If anyone does not abide in Me, he is cast out as a branch and is withered; and they gather them and throw *them* into the fire, and they are burned.

If you abide in Me, and My words abide in you, you will ask what you desire, and it shall be done for you. By this My Father is glorified, *that you bear much fruit*; so you will be My disciples. You did not choose Me, but I chose you and appointed you that you should go and *bear fruit, and that your fruit should remain*, that whatever you ask the Father in My name He may give you."

What was taking place in the Book of Acts with 3,000, 5,000, and then multitudes being added and even multiplied to the church? It was spiritual reproduction! God was working in-and-through His church to grow and perpetuate His church. Each follower of Christ did not merely exist for him/herself. There were other families to reach. There were future generations to come to know Christ (including us!). Even in spite of great persecution there was an evangelism explosion.

Therefore, those who were scattered [like seed] went everywhere preaching [evangelizing] the word. (Acts 8:4)

Just as there is a natural law of sowing and reaping, there is also a spiritual law of sowing and reaping.

The Lord spoke through the prophet Isaiah and said,

"For as the rain comes down, and the snow from heaven,
And do not return there, But water the earth,
And make it bring forth and bud,
That it may give seed to the sower And bread to the eater,

So shall My word be that goes forth from My mouth;
It shall not return to Me void,
But it shall accomplish what I please, And it shall prosper *in the thing* for which I sent it." (Isa. 55:10, 11)

God's Word provides spiritual food and energy for us ("the eater"). But it doesn't merely exist as spiritual food. It also provides seed for us ("the sower") to be sown in the hearts and lives of other individuals. Not only are we the recipients of the gospel, but we are also the sowers of the gospel.

What happens to a 50-pound bag of corn if it remains in the bag? What happens to the Seed of God's Word if it remains on the page, or we keep it to ourselves? **What happens to the Harrison Free Will Baptist Church if it stops with our generation?**

Several years ago Stan Toler wrote in his book, *The Five-Star Church*, that "more than 80% of churches in the U.S. have plateaued or are declining." Did you know that 3,500-4,000 churches close their doors every year? I would venture to say, however, that each one of these churches thought that it would never happen to them. Now tell me, what happens to a local church ifall it wants to do is consume the Word of God (constantly takes it in), but never sows the Word of God (gives it out)?

Remember this? "In some cases, once seed has been produced thus ensuring the survival of the species, the plant will stop blooming since there is no reason to put energy into blooming any longer."

Based on the theme of this article...
• Assuming we are doctrinally sound in belief and

practice, what is one thing we must we do to ensure the survival of the Harrison Free Will Baptist Church?

- Will this require energy and effort from you?
- How long will this take?

This is a quote from a message I preached on October 30, 2011: "Not only are we the product of God's purpose (redemption of a lost world), but also the means of achieving it! God redeems people for the purpose of using them to redeem other people."

Vance Havner was right: "The Gospel is not [just] something we come to church to hear; it is something we go from church to tell."
—Pastor Mike

*But this I say: He who sows sparingly will also reap sparingly, and he who sows bountifully will also reap bountifully.*~2 Cor. 10:6

# 11

## A Godly Response to an Un-godly Ruling
### *Romans 1:20-32*

---

*Shawn Beauchamp, Canaan Land Free Will Baptist*

**Intro. –**

This is NO DOUBT a topic that can stir up a lot of emotions, extreme anger ---to extreme hurt.

There will be many today who feel I am preaching too hard when talking about homosexuality and others who believe that I am not preaching hard enough. My goal today is the same as it is every Service and that is to preach and teach God's Word in a clear—yet encouraging way.

I am dealing today with this issue of HOMOSEXUALITY....as a minister of the gospel---who desires to fully follow Christ.

WHEN YOU GET A RULING ON MARRIAGE LIKE WE DID FRIDAY...THE 26

DEFENSE OF MARRIAGE AS A MAN   WOMAN IS SIMPLE WHEN IT COMES TO SCRIPTURE:

**Ephesians 5:22-33**

**Genesis 2:22-24**

**Matthew 19:**

*It used to be that homosexuals were considered to be in need of change. But now, we live in a time culture where those who oppose the homosexual lifestyle are the ones who are considered to be in need of change.*

This decision has led many to believe that Christians will run away scared  never show their face again!

I am not scared....I don't think in my heart  mind...get the kids out of public school...stop having children....who wants to bring a child in this environment?

*I quickly am reminded of verses in SCRIPTURE LIKE:*

All things work together for good, to them that love

God to those called according to His purpose....

**I Corinthians 15:58-** *Therefore, my beloved brethren, be ye stedfast, unmoveable, always abounding in the work of the Lord, forasmuch as ye know that your labour is not in vain in the Lord.*

**Psalm 34:17** - *When the righteous cry for help, the LORD hears and delivers them out of all their troubles.*

**Proverbs 3:5-6** - *Trust in the LORD with all your heart, and do not lean on your own understanding. In all your ways acknowledge him, and he will make straight your paths.*

Or let me just sing this OLD HYMN....
Trust in Him who will not leave you,
Whatsoever years may bring,
If by earthly friends forsaken
Still more closely to Him cling.

Hold to God's unchanging hand;
Build your hopes on things eternal,
Hold to God's unchanging hand.

*AS I DROVE HOME....I went through 6 STATES... I kept seeing signs that said IF WE PRAY.......I Saw a guy in Alabama with a sign in the middle of the median that said.....JESUS IS COMING.... he wasn't sad....he was smiling!!!!!*
I hope  pray that this motivates you to further study your Bible!

THIS IS AN UNPLEASANT SUBJECT...Who would have

guessed 10-15 years ago that we would be here today dealing with this issue of MARRIAGE FOR SAME –SEX COUPLES.

I want to make this very clear  plain....As a Child of God.....I     AM     PREJUDICE     CONCERNING HOMOSEXUALITY.....if that isn't plain enough......I hate it....I    make    no    apology    about that....NOW...UNDERSTAND....I   don't   hate   the HOMOSEXUAL....I hate HOMOSEXUALITY!!!!

*I WANT TO ALWAYS DISTINGUISH HATRED AS HATING THE SIN  NOT THE SINNER!!!*

It is like the fella who wanted to hate the sinner....He was talking to the Lord  said....Lord I know you told me not to hate...but if you ever make it acceptable I ALREADY HAVE THE PERSON PICKED OUT!!!!

These familiar words of EDMUND BURKE are ringing ever so clearly in my ears.....*ALL THAT IS NECESSARY FOR THE TRIUMPH OF EVIL IS THAT GOOD MEN DO NOTHING!!!*

*2 THOUGHTS that you draw from these verses*

*<u>The Tolerance of Society-</u>*

<u>*HOMOSEXUALITY    IS    A    SIN    THAT    NEEDS REPENTANCE!*</u>

Have you noticed....Mankind has always tried to make excuses  blame someone else?.....

BECAUSE OF HOME LIFE!

BECAUSE OF An unaffectionate father or an Over protective or dominate mother...***THAT WAS SIGMUND FREUD'S THEORY!***

So to deal with this.....Society says tolerate....they say...HAVE COMPASSION...The claim is that they are a Suppressed minority ....***THEIR AGENDA IS SIMPLE....THEY ARE*** Wanting SYMPATHY THEY ARE GETTING IT.....not only FROM A LIBERAL PRESS...***Liberal to me is anyone who goes against the Word of God in any form or fashion!!!---JUST FOR THE RECORD.....***

It is bad enough that these news groups special groups try to FORCE their lifestyle upon others....but that doesn't necessarily bother me or frustrate me to much.......

When SOCIETY TRIES TO CHANGE THE MEANING OF SOMETHING AS SACRED AS MARRIAGE....the very thing GOD HIMSELF INSTITUTED....MAKE NO DOUBT ABOUT IT.....GODS PEOPLE MUST ANSWER WHEN WE ANSWER....***it doesn't frustrate me*** to have the backlash from society!!!!

***It does not frustrate me*** WHEN Believers get accused of being bigoted or hate filled because in reality I KNOW....We are being loving towards others by not staying silent and allowing them to remain in error un-checked?!!!!

***It does not frustrate me***....when Homosexuals homosexual supporters rely on 1 verse of Scripture...***DO NOT JUDGE!***

*It does not frustrate me....because I know It's the responsibility of the church to teach sound doctrine* In **Ephesians 4:14-16** Paul explains the need for truth.

*14 That we henceforth be no more children, tossed to and fro, and carried about with every wind of doctrine, by the sleight of men, and cunning craftiness, whereby they lie in wait to deceive;*

*15 But speaking the truth in love, may grow up into him in all things, which is the head, even Christ:*

*16 From whom the whole body fitly joined together and compacted by that which every joint supplieth, according to the effectual working in the measure of every part, maketh increase of the body unto the edifying of itself in love.*

*It does not FRUSTRATE ME*......when I know we teach the Word of God .....IN LOVE..... *EVERYBODY engaging in that particular sin in that particular VERSE.....IS OFFENDED!!!!---It does not frustrate me...because it is easy to play the*

*"I am offended game!!!!"*

*I COULD SAY THAT I am offended:*

• That the symbol of 1 of Gods promises is the banner flag of a perverted lifestyle

• That 5 people who think they are more educated in Law will think they answer for those who are educated in God's Word being labeled...OFFENSSIVE.... does not frustrate me:

*Here is what is frustrating to me: it is one thing for the world to promote the homosexual lifestyle as acceptable, but I find it disturbing FRUSTRATING when I hear of those who claim to be Christians saying that there is nothing wrong with it.*

What bothers me as a PREACHER is churches that sympathize even agree with this CONCEPT OF LOVE!

*What bothers me as an ORDAINED MINISTER CALLED BY GOD TO PREACH THE WHOLE COUNSEL OF GOD IS that.......talk of SYMPATHY has replaced the talk OF SIN from many pulpits!!!*

Many will ask....how can this be happening in **churches**. I can tell you how.... because a great many leaders who stand in pulpits....no longer accept the Bible as God"s Word and thus pay no attention to its teaching on homosexuality. As one minister has said, *"We have learned not to get hung up on the Bible."*

Supposed Believers base their decision of HOMOSEXUALITY on a friend that is HOMOSEXUAL or family member that is HOMOSEXUAL....or many refuse to bring someone to church because they are afraid of what the preacher might say.....IF THIS IS YOU YOU FALL IN THIS PARTICULAR CATEGORY.....YOU SHOULD BE ASHAMED OF YOURSELF!!!!---- *IF YOU ARE A PROFESSED CHRISTIAN THEY DON'T KNOW WHERE YOU STAND.... YOU HAVENT MADE IT CLEAR WHERE YOU STAND.....YOU SHOULD BE ASHAMED!!!!*

But Many TO BE HONEST....do not stand because they don't have a clear grasp of scripture concerning this SIN....---BE REMINDED TODAY...WE CANNOT BE

TOLERANT                                                    OF
HOMOSEXUALITY...BECAUSE.....*HOMOSEXUALITY ISNT SIMPLY A LIFESTYLE....IT IS A SIN!!!*

They call this COMING OUT this BOLDNESS a sign of FREEDOM   HONESTY of who they really are.....THEY DON'T EVEN BLUSH...<u>Jeremiah 6:15</u> says *Were they ashamed when they had committed abomination? nay, they were not at all ashamed, neither could they blush: therefore they shall fall among them that fall: at the time that I visit them they shall be cast down, saith the Lord.*

The BIBLE says this is a sign of a civilization that is *decaying*!---one who sins but does not blush!!!!

MARK TWAIN WROTE: *Man is the only animal that blushes BECAUSE it is the only animal that needs to.*

THIS AGENDA of tolerance HAS HAD SUCCESS IN MANY CHURCHES IN OUR AREA!

30 DIFFERENT CHURCHES IN THE COLUMBUS AREA --- PROMOTE a GAY LIFESTYLE  HOW THEY CAN SERVE GOD IN THE CHURCH (Gaychurch.org)....*UNDERSTAND: we do not turn anyone away from COMING to church.....EVERYONE IS WELCOME To hear the Gospel....BUT...only a blood boutght Child of God HAS THE RIGHT TO SERVE!!!!*

*THIS RULING HAS PAVED THE WAY TO FORCE CHURCHES WHO DISAGREE TO COMPLY.....BUT LET ME SAY THIS:*

---The White House may say Gay Marriage is a victory for AMERICA

---The Court House may issue a MARRIAGE LICENSE

---BUT....Gods House will always be different!!!

WHY? IT IS SIMPLE.....*CHRIST ISNT RETURNING FOR A CHURCH THAT PROMOTES GAY PRIDE....HE IS RETURNING FOR A CHURCH THAT IS A PURE BRIDE!!!!-*-----STICK THAT ON A SHIRT OR A BUMPER STICKER!!!!!

When someone announces they are GAY....they ask for COMPASSION

When someone announces they are a child of God .....They are considered a bigot!

THEY WILL CALL GOOD EVIL... EVIL GOOD!!!- that is what **Isaiah 5:20 says!**

Is Homosexuality a sin? ----

**Genesis 1:27**- no one was created a HOMOSEXUAL!

Leviticus 18:22- Pretty Clear

Leviticus 20:13- Deuteronomy 22:5

Scripture is opposed to Homosexuality and classifies it as a SIN!

Society wants TOLERANCE - SYMPATHY!!!!

*Homosexuality IS A CHOICE! Meaning: it is a LEARNED BEHAVIOR!*

*SYMPATHY IS WHAT THEY WANT..... TOLERANCE IS WHAT THEY WANT.....THESE ARE* .....All part of the Devils plan to make Homosexuality acceptable!!!

The Bible clearly says.....***Be not conformed to this world but be ye transformed by the renewing of you mind.....***

WELL, THOSE ARE OLD TESTAMENT PASSAGES....THOU SHALT NOT KILL THOU SHALT NOT STEAL IS IN THE OT TOO...SHOULD WE FORGET THOSE AS WELL?

**Read Romans 1:20-32!!!**

Listen: it does not take a SEMINARY GRADUATE to figure out what is going on in this portion of scripture Paul is writing!!!!

**SOCIETY SAYS.....THIS IS SICKNESS....THIS IS HEREDITARY—YOU ARE BORN THIS WAY!--- THEY WANT L...**TOLERANCE BECAUSE THEY ARE BORN THIS WAY!!!!

Don't be naïve....Homosexuals are not born this way.....***IT IS STILL A CHOICE!!***

***Homosexual isn't what a person IS....it is something a person DOES***.....otherwise God would not CALL IT A SIN WORTHY OF DEATH!!!!

***GUY CHARLES---37 YEARS A HOMOSEXUAL who was saved*** told a correspondent for a national newspaper these words, "Nobody is born gay. You are born male or female, and the conditioning you receive as you grow up shapes your sexual development. At some point in our lives, **we make a decision** either physically or mentally to participate in a sexual act. The decision is repeated over and over until it's a habit, and the habit forms the lifestyle." And then once you've chosen that lifestyle, they say you develop the mannerisms to appeal to other sodomites.

DID YOU GET THAT? A HOMOSEXUAL WHO CONVERTED TO CHRISTIANITY SAID:

Homosexuality is an act of the will...which becomes a habit ...... So it is a sin that needs to be repented of... BUT IF YOU DO NOT SAY IT IS SIN.....BECAUSE YOU "LOVE THEM"—LET ME REMIND YOU:

**When you act as if there isn't a problem---- you deny they need a cure.**

These HOMOSEXUAL mannerisms are learned TRAITS and are encouraged in the gay community to try to make it normalized!!!!...They do not have EXTRA female hormones or a chemical imbalance --- They are traits that are learned --- they are learned in order to attract **another homosexual.**

No science OF ANY KIND has never been able to prove contrary to this. There has never been a GAY GENE ----- **people are HOMOSEXUALS for no other reason other than they choose to   when this choice is made GOD CALLS IT SIN!!!!!**

let me throw this in....for good measure....ANY STUDY THAT CONDONES HOMOSEXUALITY has been conducted or funded by....GUESS WHO? **YOU GOT**

*IT....HOMOSEXUALS!!!!—TO BIASELY CHANGE THE PERCEPTION OF THE UNINFORMED!*

The Word of God loudly proclaims that Homosexuality is wrong....not because we don't love the sinner....but because we love them enough to tell the truth in order for them to see that what they are doing is SIN!!!!

THAT IS WHY THE CHURCH STRONGLY OPPOSE'S DOES NOT TOLERATE HOMOSEXUALITY.....

*To tolerate today....is to encourage in the future*

*Bell and Weinberg, did a study of male and female homosexuality, many years ago...they found that 43 percent of white male homosexuals had sex with 500 or more partners, with 28 percent having one thousand or more sex partners.*

*Domestic violence is higher in HOMOSEXUALS- http://winteryknight.com/2013/11/18/domestic- violence-rates-are-higher-for-homosexual-couples- than-for-heterosexual-couples/*

*Familiarity does not breed contempt....Familiarity breeds TOLERANCE*

We can let OUR CHILDREN be bombarded surrounded with....TV, INTERNET, PHONES, SCHOOL, RADIO

And act like it isn't affecting them.....but make no mistake....

*WE ARE WHAT WE SEE,   WHAT WE THINK   WHAT*

*WE HEAR….Homosexuals cannot REPRODUCE so they RECRUIT!!!*

IT IS A FACT THAT…..YOUNGER CHILDREN IS THEIR FAVORITE           TARGET!!!!---Because           they know……*CHILDREN COPY THE BEHAVIORS THEY SEE!!!!!!*

***This is how many churches of today respond….THEY DON'T FACE IT HEAD ON     SAY IT IS SIN….THEY TOLERATE IT!!!!!***

**2 Timothy 3:1-5***This know also, that in the last days perilous times shall come.*

*2 For men shall be lovers of their own selves, covetous, boasters, proud, blasphemers, disobedient to parents, unthankful, unholy,*

*3 Without natural affection, trucebreakers, false accusers, incontinent, fierce, despisers of those that are good,*

*4 Traitors, heady, high-minded, lovers of pleasures more than lovers of God;*

*5 Having a form of godliness, but denying the power thereof: from such turn away.*

*THE DECISION MANY WANT TO BELIEVE …..IS BASED ON THE FACT THAT TIMES HAVE CHANGED….BUT LET ME REMIND THE 5 JUDGES AS WELL AS THOSE WHO THINK THEY HAVE GAINED A VICTORY OF SOME*

*SORT........TIMES MAY HAVE CHANGED....PEOPLE'S OPINION MAY HAVE CHANGED....BUT GOD HASN'T NEITHER HAS HIS WORD!!!!!*

*In order to receive the forgiveness of God, the sinner has to see what they are doing is a sin.*

*Calling it SOMETHING OTHER THAN SIN is DENYING THE SIN  DAMNING THEIR SOUL!!!! When you endorse this AGENDA....YOU ARENT HELPING THEM AT ALL....you are saying there choices  actions are not SIN!!!!---GOD HELP YOUR SOUL!!!!!*

*IF YOU WANT TO EMPTY A CHURCH OF GODS POWER  BLESSING---JUST START APPROVING SAME – SEX MARRIAGE!!!*

*Oh, you may have a crowd....but God will not be in the midst!!!!!*

I want you to understand...we love the sinner here at this church....but we will not tolerate open sin!......*Here @ our church we will oppose it...we will teach  preach against it...we will stand against it... we will not tolerate it for 1 second!!!!!*

*For if we tolerate what the Word of God says is SIN....we are like the church at EPHESUS, PERGAMUM, THYATIRA ALL ROLLED INTO ONE!!!*

Here is the reasoning of TOLERANCE......*Story of bad driver* ....there was a boy who got a car in our subdivision ...he comes roaring through there....squealing hisl tires....I hate it...because my children are around there playing all the time!!!....I

CAUGHT HIM!!!....I told him kindly....I don't like what you are doing Because He endangers the lives of my children....,NOW...many said....YOU SHOULD BE TOLERANT? You don't know his home life...you don't know what he is going through....he has had a bad year.......BE COMPASSIONATE....BE TOLERANT....DONT SAY ANYTHING THAT ISNT NICE!!!!

I said something.... would say something again if needed...yes EVEN when others wouldn't......*DO YOU KNOW WHY?* .....IT IS BECAUSE THEY DON'T LOVE MY CHILDREN LIKE I DO!!!!!! *IF YOU TELL ME TO BE TOLERANT OF SIN....YOU DON'T LOVE THIS CHURCH LIKE I DO!!!!!---*

People say...quit preaching on sin.....be tolerant....*HEAR IT HEAR IT GOOD*.....*Tolerance isn't having compassion....TOLERANCE is A LACK OF CONCERN!!!*

*JOHN OWENS says it this way....He who has thoughts of sin....NEVER had great thoughts of God!*

*So what they are trying to do is BULLY INTIMIDATE the church of the Lord Jesus Christ to go away accept and hide and be quiet!!!*

*But here is their IGNORANCE -------YOU CANNOT SILENCE THE WORD OF GOD!!!!!*

*SO WE SEE:*

*<u>The Tolerance of Society-</u>*

*<u>The Teachings of God</u>*

**THE TEACHINGS OF GOD SHOWS US:** *FAMILY IS A FATHER MOTHER-* Gen. 2:24

God made Eve for Adam. A PERFECT HELP......This is God"s design for the family. The creation of men and women *differently* IN ORDER to fulfill specific roles within the family. Now I know WE HAVE there single PARENTS that do a great job of raising their children, *but God has designed the family to function best with a MOTHER FATHER--TOGETHER.* Even though Jesus did not address the issue of homosexuality specifically, *When Christ spoke in reference to marriage, ---it ALWAYS....involved a man and a woman.* THE PROOF IS IN Matthew 19:5.....He quotes **Genesis 2:24** as the EVERLASTING ---NEVER CHANGING nature of the marriage bond----So the trend today for states to allow gay marriage is wrong *because it goes against God"s design for what He has said makes as the definition of the family.*

**THE TEACHINGS OF GOD SHOW US: THE true FAMILY---but also....TRUE FREEDOM**

**FREEDOM IS FOUND ONLY in Christ Jesus!**

DO YOU REALIZE WHEN CHRIST DIED ON THE CROSS HE DIED FOR HOMOSEXUAL SINS TOO?

We applaud everyone who recovers or turns away from every other sin....alcohol, adultery, fornication drug addicts ....but Homosexuals are sent away!

**I Corinthians 6:9-10** *Know ye not that the unrighteous shall not inherit the kingdom of God? Be not deceived: neither fornicators, nor idolaters, nor* *adulterers, nor effeminate, nor abusers of themselves with mankind, 10 Nor thieves, nor covetous, nor drunkards, nor revilers, nor extortioners, shall inherit the kingdom of God.*

*UNDERSTAND: PAUL IS WRITING THIS....this had happened in the Corinthian church.*

*THE PROBLEM of sin....IS FOUND IN VS. 9-10......but THE FREEDOM from SIN....IS FOUND IN VS. 11*

*11 And such were some of you: but ye are washed, but ye are sanctified, but ye are justified in the name of the Lord Jesus, and by the Spirit of our God.*

*THESE CORNITHIANS WERE EX- EVERY SIN LISED IN VERSES 9   10!!!!*

*SO IF THEY are redeemable. If they can be saved. If....They can be delivered from that sin. If ....They can be washed from in the blood of the Lamb their life be changed.....IF THEY CAN BE A WERE....SO CAN fornicators today...so can Idolaters today....so can HOMOSEXUALS today..... They just have to see that it is truly SIN!!!!*

*The Corinthian church was full of those kinds of people, and so is OUR Church.—A WHOLE BUNCH OF WERE'S!*

*THIS IS MY PRAYER------That this RULING awaken God's people!!!!!*

*Understand.....CHRISTIAN....The culture may be crumbling. But the church isn't SHAKING!!!*

*God is still on His throne and the gospel of Jesus Christ still SAVES TODAY..... America is SAID TO BE the new Rome. But if I remember correctly.....Rome is where the church exploded in growth!!!!!. REMEMBER CHRISTIAN.....*

*We should have no problem....taking a stand*

*We should have no problem as a blood bought Child of the living God.....running into the battle.*

*IN THE DAYS OF THE PIONEERS WHEN MEN WOULD SEE THAT A PRAIRIE FIRE WAS COMING, DO YOU KNOW WHAT THEY WOULD DO? SINCE NOT EVEN THE FASTEST OF HORSES COULD OUTRUN A PRAIRIE FIRE, THE PIONEERS WOULD TAKE A MATCH AND BURN THE GRASS IN A DESIGNATED AREA AROUND THEM. THEN THEY WOULD TAKE THEIR STAND IN THE BURNED AREA, KNOWING THEY WOULD BE SAFE FROM THE FIRE. AS THE ROAR OF THOSE FLAMES GOT CLOSER AND CLOSER, THEY WOULD NOT EVEN FLINCH. THE REASON? BECAUSE FIRE CANNOT COME WHERE FIRE HAS ALREADY BEEN.*

*WHEN THE FIRE OF GODS JUDGMENT FALLS ONCE AGAIN ON THIS WORLD, THERE WILL ONLY BE ONE SPOT WHERE IT IS SAFE TO STAND, AND THAT IS AT THE CROSS OF THE LORD JESUS CHRIST, WHERE THE FIRE OF GODS JUDGMENT HAS ALREADY FALLEN. I HOPE YOU WILL KEEP THAT IN MIND ....*

*The answer TO HOMOSEXUALITY is....*

*STRONG CHRISTIAN HOMES....HOMES WHERE YOUNG MEN ARE TAUGHT TO BE MASCULINE.... YOUNG*

*WOMAN ARE FEMININE!!!!! You make your family so strong   so good that people who may not live this way....will look to the Christian lifestyle   emulate us....instead of them!!!*

*FAMILIES....MOMS       DADS....Will you join this movement? Will you come join this church and establish this promise to God?*

*If you aren't a Christian....you had better choose...*

*JOSHUA SAID (24:15)... And if it seem evil unto you to serve the LORD, choose you this day whom ye will serve; whether the gods which your fathers served that were on the other side of the flood, or the gods of the Amorites, in whose land ye dwell: but as for me and my house, we will serve the LORD.*

*QUIT STRATTLING THE FENCE....ARE YOU FOR CHRIST OR AGAINST HIM?*

*If you are unsaved...it is time to be a WERE as Paul puts it....families...it is time to decide....whether your family will be a spectator OF THE BATTLE....or a devoted follower of Christ IN THE BATTLE!!!!*

# 12

## How Do You Build A Great Church?

---

### Alton Loveless, Retired

Acts 2:42-47

*And they continued stedfastly in the <u>apostles' doctrine</u> and fellowship, and in breaking of bread, and in prayers.*

*[43] And fear came upon every soul: and many wonders and signs were done by the apostles.*

*[44] And all that believed were together, and had all things common;*

*[45] And sold their possessions and goods, and parted them to all men, as every man had need.*

*[46] And they, continuing daily with one accord in the temple, and breaking bread from house to house, did eat their meat with gladness and singleness of heart,*

*[47] Praising God, and having favour with all the people.*

---

*And the Lord added to the church daily such as should be saved.*

## I.   You build a great church with a great preacher

You cannot be anything if you want to be everything. Solomon Schechter (1847-1915)

There are countless words in the Bible for Leadership

Luke 4:18

The Spirit of the Lord is upon me, because he hath anointed me to preach the gospel to the poor; he hath sent me to heal the brokenhearted, to preach deliverance to the captives, and recovering of sight to the blind, to set at liberty them that are bruised,

A.   Episkapos – <u>Ephes. 4:11</u> And he gave some, apostles; and some, prophets; and some, evangelists; and some, pastors and teachers;

B.   Presbuteros – 1 Tim. 3:1 This is a true saying, If a man desire the office of a bishop, he desireth a good work.

C.   Poimen – Feeder of the flock - <u>Acts 20:28</u> Take heed therefore unto yourselves, and to all the flock, over which the Holy Ghost hath made you overseers, to feed the church of God, which he hath purchased with his own blood.

## II.    You Build A Great Church With A Great People

Philip. 1:1 -- *Paul and Timotheus, the servants of Jesus Christ, to all the saints in Christ Jesus which are at Philippi, with the <u>bishops and deacons</u>:*

*Romans 12:7 -- Or ministry, let us wait on our ministering: or he that teacheth, on teaching;*

    A.    Diakonos ("To stir up the Dust")
    B.    Fellowship, Relationship, Discipleship, Worship, Followship

    C.    Determined    – Heped up

          Dedicated    – Humbled

          Dependable    – Happy

          Saved    – Called out

          Sanctified    – Called in

          Separated    – Called up

*O Lord, help us to be thankful that you have "not dealt with us after our sins; nor rewarded us according to our iniquities* (Psa. 103:10).

<u>This world is God's house</u>. He's left clues everywhere about what kind of God he is.

When you stand at the Grand Canyon, you can't help but be overwhelmed at the mighty power of God to create such magnificence. He must have had a mighty hand to scoop out the Royal Gorge in Colorado.

He is as infinite as the dark recesses of the mighty Atlantic Ocean.

Each snowflake testifies to his uniqueness.

The changing colors of the Great Smoky Mountains proclaim his creativity.

The galaxies shout out, "He is there."

The wildflowers sing together, "He is there."

The rippling brooks join in, "He is there."

The birds sing it, the lions roar it, the fish write it in the oceans—"He is there."

All creation joins to sing his praise.

The heavens declare it, the earth repeats it and the wind whispers it—"He is there."

Deep cries out to deep,

The mighty sequoia tells it to the eagle who soars overhead,

The lamb and the wolf agree on this one thing—"He is there."

No one can miss the message. God has left his fingerprints all over this world. Truly, "This is my Father's world," and every rock, every twig, every river and every mountain bears his signature. He signed his name to everything he made. The earth is marked "Made By God" in letters so big that no one fails to see it. *"The heavens declare the glory of God; the skies proclaim the work of his hands"* (Psalm 19:1).

To call him the Father Almighty means that we can trust him in every circumstance because he will do whatever needs to be done to take care of us.

Romans 8:31-32 expresses this truth beautifully: *"What, then, shall we say in response to this? If God is for us, who can be against us? He who did not spare his own Son, but gave him up for us all—how will he not also, along with him, graciously give us all things?"*

What is the limit of the "all things" in verse 32? Answer: There is no limit.

Whatever we truly need, our Father will make sure that we have it because he is the "Father Almighty." His name is El Shaddai—Almighty God.

### III. You Build A Great Church With A Great Passion

A. "Look on the Fields...White unto Harvest.

- Motion without movement

- Vision without victory

- Religion without revival

- Spirituality without Salvation

- Doxology without Devotion

- Cause without Cure

- Sadness without Sight

- Prayer without Power

- Enthusiasm without Examination

- Profession without procession

B.   After Pentecost they were translated to perform

- Experiences into Expeditions

- Cleansing into Campaigning

- Worship into work

- Communion into commission

C.   120,000,000 were in the Roman Empire at the time.

       i. 120 disciples in the upper room...500 invited

      ii. But the Holy Spirit overwhelmed those that came

- Religious Bigotry in Jerusalem

- Materialism in Ephesus

- Military Might of Rome

- Idolatry of Athens

- Intellectualism of Greece

- Rationalism of Sadducees

- Ritualism of Pharisees

Half the known world was saved before Paul's death.

Scaffolds became pulpits

Coliseums became witness stands

Sign of the Fish

The three foundational documents of the Christian church—

The Ten Commandments, The Lord's Prayer, And The Apostles' Creed.

THE APOSTLES' CREEDI believe in God, the Father Almighty, the Creator of heaven and earth, and in Jesus Christ, his only son, our Lord: Who was conceived of the Holy Spirit, born of the Virgin Mary, suffered under Pontius Pilate, was crucified, died, and was buried. He descended into hell. The third day he rose again from the dead. He ascended into heaven and sits at the right hand of the Father Almighty, whence he shall come to judge the living and the dead. I believe in the Holy Spirit, the holy Christian church, the communion of saints, the forgiveness of sins, the resurrection of the body, and life everlasting. Amen.

- The Creed reminds us that truth is not optional.

- There are boundaries to the Christian faith.

- Not everything is negotiable.

Some things must be believed if you are to call yourself a Christian.

You can choose to live outside those boundaries, but if you do, you aren't a Christian and you shouldn't call yourself one.

This leads us to a vital truth point: Christianity is a doctrinal faith. It is not an "X" that you can fill in with whatever content you desire.

Note that when the Creed calls God the "Maker of heaven and earth," it parts company with Hinduism and by extension, with all the Eastern religions.

When it declares that Jesus is the Christ, God's only Son, and our Lord, it parts company with Islam and Judaism. This claim for Jesus makes Christianity utterly unique.

These titles were commonly used by the early church to describe their faith. Sometimes they used the familiar symbol of the fish, which in Greek is IXTHUS. Those letters were an acrostic for four of the words found in this phrase of the Creed:

- The letter I is the first letter of "Jesus" in Greek.

- The letter X is the first letter of "Christ" in Greek.

- The letters TH stand for the first letter of "God" in Greek.

- The letter U is the first letter of "Son" in Greek.

- The letter S is the first letter of "Savior" in Greek.

- So the word IXTHUS (and the fish symbol) stood as shorthand for: Jesus Christ, God's Son, our Savior.

What have we learned from the Scriptures?

- Old Testament—Anticipation

- Gospels—Incarnation

- Acts—Proclamation

- Epistles—Explanation

- Revelation—Consummation

The Old Testament says, "He is coming!"

- The Gospels say, "He is here!"

- The book of Acts says, "He has come!"

- The Epistles say, "He is Lord!"

- Revelation says, "He is coming again!"

## IV. You Build A Great Church With A Great Program

To quote Buddha, He once said that if one person conquers in battle a thousand times a thousand and another conquers himself, he who conquers himself is the greatest of all conquerors. But how much do we know about self-conquest, self-mastery, and self-control? Why do I say that love is balanced by self-control? Because love is self-giving, and self-giving and self-control are complementary, the one to the other. How can we give ourselves in love until we've learned to control ourselves? Our self has to be mastered before it can be offered in the service of others.

-- John Stott, "A Vision for Holiness," Preaching Today

| A. | M | ethods |
|----|---|--------|
|    | O | bjective |
|    | D | ependence |
|    | E | nthusiasm |
|    | L | ife |

B. Revival..

- A revival breaks the power of the world and the sin over the Christian.

- Revival...Always begins a new beginning of obedience to God.

C. A Revival may be expected when:

      1.    The providence of God indicates a revival is at hand.

      2.    The wickedness of the wicked grieves and humbles and distresses the Christian.

      3.    When Christian have a spirit of prayer for Revival

      4.    When Christians begin to confess their sins one to another.

      5.    When every ones attention is directed toward revival.

      6.    When Christians are found willing to make sacrifice necessary to carry it on.

      7.    When Christians are willing to have God Promote it by what instrumentals He pleases.

My relationship with God is part of my relationship with men. Failure in one will cause failure with the other.

-- Andrew Murray in With Christ in the School of Prayer. Christianity Today, Vol. 35, no. 5.

D.    Hindrances to Revival

1.    A revival will cease when Christians become mechanical in the attempt to promote it.

2.    A Revival will cease when Christians get the idea the work will go on without them.

3.    A revival will cease when the Church prefers to attend to its own concerns rather that God's business

4.    A revival will cease when Christians refuse to render to the Lord according to the benefits received.

# 13

## REVIEWING THE PRESENT

---

Dr. Alton E. Loveless
Columbus, Ohio

Tonight I feel awesome being placed between a President Emeritus and a Preacher A-merited, since I was always a Pupil de-merited!

I feel much like the puffed up student selected by a group of professors to be taught all they knew about the flood. After weeks of intense teaching and training they were ready to send them to lecture to others. Noticing his conceitedness and haughty spirit felt he needed deflated before he left decided to tell him the following, "We have taught you all we know. You have the combined knowledge of those of us who have been your mentors. You know more than anyone we know about the flood. However, we feel you should know that where you will be speaking tomorrow at your first lecture you will have a very special guest we haven't even met. Noah will be there!"

I feel much the same way as I view the countless mentors, teacher, and leaders who grace this 50th Golden Anniversary.

My subject "REVIEWING THE PRESENT" is greatly influenced by a survey mailed to pastors in every conference of our National Association. Seventy-seven responses were received from this mailing representing 25 states and Canada. It represented large and small churches, city and rural, north and south, east and west. All responses were from pastors with a combined ministry of 1,681 years of service. The average age was 45 with the youngest being 27 and the oldest 67. They averaged beginning to preach at age 24 and oddly enough, while all pastors were selected at random from the national directory, the academic background averaged 4 years of college with 61 having attended college and 16 not having that privilege. The least educated had completed the 6th grade and the highest attained was 7 years of college. (Perhaps college men are more accustomed to surveys the reason for their greater response). Sixty (60) were full-time with 17 others supplementing their income. Of the respondents 57 said their church was growing and 20 said no. The average membership of their churches was 179 with the largest having 1,350 members and the smallest 20. They averaged 133 in attendance. Forty-six (46) said the attitude of their people toward church growth was average to good but 12 classified their churches attitude as excellent. Nineteen was poor to average.

Probably the most referred to item centered around leadership as being our key problem from Pastor, Membership, and routing itself to our National. Most pastors felt deficient in themselves and were seeking help from a national leadership they felt weak and divided without common goals.

Raymond C. Ortlund in his book, LET THE CHURCH BE THE CHURCH, tells of a pilot who announced over his intercom system, "Ladies and gentlemen, I have good news and bad news. The good news in that we have a tailwind and are making excellent time. The bad news is that our compass is broken and we have no idea where we are going."

There is a story in THE LAST HURRAH that illustrates my concern. The mayor of Boston is watching a parade. He says, "There go the people. I am their leader. I must follow them."

Since no one rises higher than leadership takes us, I feel it helpful that we look at the men the Master chose and how He developed leadership. How could Christ take 12 of the most changeable men and move the world. How could Jesus who knows all things make such a mistake in choosing such men of diversity?

May I suggest from the beginning that these were His best friends. And while we are concerned about being his friend we forget these were His whom He had called to train. They, like us, broke His heart many times as He sought to make them leaders.

Most of you probably cannot name all twelve of these men but they appear in the Bible in four different places as an entire group. (Matthew 10:2, 3; Mark 3:16-19; Luke 6:14-16; and Acts 1:13).

Please note that in all four lists Simon Peter is always listed first. Judas always appears last in the lists except in Acts where he has already betrayed the Lord. Note the disciples appear in all four lists in three groups of four. It is interesting to note the same person appears first in each of the three groups. Peter in group one; Phillip in group two; James the Less in group three.

They also must have had a partner as well. This is indicated from Mark 6:7 as they were sent out two by two. Sometime in your study observe who ran around with whom.
I believe I can fairly classify these three groups:

**Group one:**
The Presenters - The Vocal Ones - Authoritarian Leaders
**Group two:**
The Contenders - The Varied Ones - The Automatic Leaders
**Group three:**
The Pretenders - The Vacillating One's - Appointed Leaders

Matthew 9:35-10:7, *"And Jesus went about all the cities and villages, teaching in their synagogues, and preaching the gospel of the kingdom, and healing every sickness and every disease among the people. But when he saw the multitudes, he was moved with compassion on them, because they fainted, and were scattered abroad, as sheep having no shepherd. Then saith he unto his disciples, The harvest truly is plenteous, but the labourers are few; Pray ye therefore the Lord of the harvest, that he will send forth labourers into his harvest. And when he had called unto him his twelve disciples, he gave them power against unclean spirits, to cast them out, and to heal all manner of sickness and all manner of disease. Now the names of the twelve apostles are these; The first, Simon, who is called Peter, and Andrew his brother; James the Son of Zebedee, and John his brother; Philip, and Bartholomew; Thomas, and Matthew the publican; James the son of Alphaeus, and Lebbaeus, whose surname was Thaddasus; Simon the Canaanite, and Judas Iscariot, who also betrayed him. These twelve Jesus sent forth, and commanded them, saying, Go not into the way of the Gentiles, and into any city of the Samaritans enter ye not; But go rather to the lost sheep of the house of Israel. And as ye go, preach, saying, The kingdom of heaven is at hand."*

## I. THE PRESENTERS - THE VOCAL ONES - AUTHORITARIAN LEADERS

The first disciple I will refer to is SIMON PETER.

He was THE OUTFRONT ONE but he was TESTED BY SPIRITUAL INVENTORY.

Simon Peter is what students of leadership would call a task oriented leader. The text called him the first Simon. He was not first by order of calling, but rather because he was always the up-front, out-front man. The Greek word "protos" is used for first in this verse. The same word is used in I Timothy 4:15 for chief, *"This is a faithful saying and worthy of all acceptation, that Christ Jesus came into the world to save sinners; of whom I am chief."*

Simon Peter, we know more about him than most all the other disciples. Next to the name of Jesus, Peter appears more than any other disciple in the gospels. No disciple speaks as often as Peter and nobody is spoken to by the Lord as often as Peter. He is reproved by the Lord. No one acknowledges the

Lordship of Christ as boldly as Peter, yet no one so boldly denied it as Peter.

He has three unusual characteristics:
a. Inquisitive. Peter asks more questions in the Gospels than all the other disciples combined.

- How often should I forgive? (Matthew 18:21).
- What reward will we get if we follow? (Matthew 19:27).
- What about the fig tree that has withered? (Mark 11:21).
- What about the meaning of the ned? (Mark 13:3).

b. Initiative. Peter not only asked questions but he was always the one who answered.

- When Jesus asked, *"Who touched me?"* (Luke 8:45) Peter answered.
- When Jesus asked, *"Who say ye that I am?"* (Matthew 16:15-16) Peter answered.
- When Jesus asked, *"Will you also go away..."* (John 6:67) Peter said, *"To whom shall we go...you have the word of eternal life."*

c. Involved. Leaders are always in the middle of everything.

- Matthew 14:29. Peter jumped out of the boat and walked on the water. We criticize him for lack of faith but six others didn't have enough to even jump in.

- Peter denied Christ 3 times, but none of the others were there. .Earlier the men *"left all and followed Him"* but now they *"forsook Him and fled."*
- After the resurrection, John stood at the entrance of the tomb, but Peter rushed right in.

**Second he was TAINTED BY SECULAR IDENTIFICATION.**

In John 1:42 Jesus at His first meeting of Simon said, *"Thou art Simon the son of Jona: Thou shalt be called Cephas, which is by interpretation, a stone."*

Simon was the name used when he was referred to by SECULAR identification.

- The house of Simon (Mark 1:29).
- Simon's wife's mother (Mark 1:30; Luke 4:38).
- Simon's boat (Luke 5:3).
- Simon's fishing partners (Luke 5:10).
- Simon's house (Luke 4:38, Acts 10:17).

When Jesus reprimanded him for SIN he was also called Simon. Luke 5:4-5, *"He said unto Simon, launch out into the deep, and let down your nets for a draught, and Simon answering said unto him, Master, we have toiled all the night, and have taken nothing. Nevertheless at thy word I will let down the net."* He is saying, This is ridiculous! We are the professionals. He is just a carpenter, O well. Luke 5:8.. *"Depart from me; for I am a sinful man, O Lord."*

Three times Jesus asked him, *"Simon, son of Jonah, lovest thou me?"*

However, when Jesus builds him up, He calls him Peter.

Thirdly, notice he is TAUGHT BY SPIRITUAL INSISTENCE. Vocal leaders often pay dearly. Simon Peter did. You cannot know the impetuous,       changeable Simon until you read his two little epistles in the back of the new Testament. Then you will see "The stone." Vocal leaders would do well to study the life of Simon Peter's inconsistency.

**The second disciple I want to consider is ANDREW who I call THE MANLY ONE.**

First, note he was A TESTIFIER BECAUSE OF SPIRITUAL INCREASE. Andrew, whose name means "manly," never broke into the inner circle. Only once is he ever listed with the other three in a group and that is in Mark 13:3 when they sat upon the Mount Olives and asked Jesus, *"Tell us when shall these things be: and what shall be the sign when all these things shall be fulfilled?"*

Andrew was never as out front or forward as his brother. (By the way, how would you always like to be referred to as someone's brother?) All, but one time, Andrew is referred to as Simon Peter's brother. In fact, he is not mentioned in any detail in the first three gospels (his calling, etc.), but in the Gospel of John he is mentioned in three distinct instances and in each he is doing the same thing. He was bringing people to Jesus.

- John 1:40-42a: He brought Peter to Christ.
- John 6:8-9: He brought the little boy with fish and loaves.
- John 12:20-22: He brought the Greeks to Christ.

Thank God there dwells among our denomination men still interested in bringing men to Christ. Soul winners who remain unsung and whose churches are growing. However, we need to be careful that our pride of success does not lead us to:

**A TEMPTATION DUE TO SATANIC INTERVENTION.**

C.S. Lewis said, "The Source of pride is comparison."

History reveals few great churches exist from times past and they are only a shadow of its greatness. Time is our greatest enemy. You may have a great church today and you should preach for its very soul for growth. But wait a little while. Give Satan time, your people time, your pride time. But be aware men die, movements fade, monuments fall, and only the message falters not. The flood of Hell cannot prevail upon the church of Jesus Christ.

Our greatest failure is to see things as physical, not spiritual; earthly, not heavenly; as time, not eternal. We are nearsighted, out of focus; blind to our own conceits; boastful in our own capabilities; and burdened by our own carelessness. We have a tendency to: view with human eyes and dim the eye of faith; to weigh things on the world's scales, not on eternity's balances; and to obscure present realities with pipedreams, or fantasies, instead of giving ourselves with courage and faith to changing this world for Christ.

**Remember, "History is His story and we have little regard for it."**

**The third disciple in this group is JAMES who I will called THE "HOT HEAD for obvious reasons.**

James **WAS TEMPERAMENTAL BY IMPLICATION**. Note that James' name always appears before his brother John in the gospels. Perhaps he was the elder or the one of stronger influence. James was a fiery fellow evidence by Luke (;51-56, *"And it came to pass, when the time was come that he should be received up, he steadfastly set his face to go to Jerusalem, And sent messengers before his face: and they went, and entered into a village of the Samaritans, to make ready for him. And they did not receive him, because his face was as though he would go to Jerusalem. And when his disciples James and John saw this, they said, Lord, wilt thou that we command fire to come down from heaven, and consume them, even as Elias did? But he turned, and rebuked them, and said, Ye know not what manner of spirit ye are of. For the Son of man is not come to destroy men's lives, but to save them. And they went to another village.*

"Let us pray that fire come from Heaven." I do not believe they would make good missionaries. Do you? Note Jesus rebuked them. In Mark 3:17, Jesus called "them Boanerges, Sons of thunder."

James had a **TEMPORARY MESSAGE DUE TO IMPRISONMENT. T**he only place James appears without John is in Acts 12:1-4 when Herod subdues this zealous, aggressive, passionate, fervent man by taking his head. This occurs only 14 years after he wanted to know on which side of the Lord he would sit in the kingdom.

Now let me consider **JOHN - THE BELOVED DISCIPLE.**

John is also charged with **A TANTRUM OF INDICTMENT.** The only time we find John alone in the

Gospels is in Mark 9:38 and he is upset. *"Master, we saw one casting out devils in thy name, and he followed not us: and we forbade him, because he followeth not us. "* At this time he was still sectarian, narrow-minded, unbending, and intolerant.

My how we need to work on this. We are a diverse denomination. Born out of it. Still in it! Can't we be diverse without being divisive?

One respondent stated, "our problem is the vocal minority is unwilling to accept the diversity of our many." More than half of the replies from my poll made mention of our: Lack of togetherness, Division, Intolerance of each other, Lack of brotherly love, Suspicion and jealousy, Lack of doctrinal purity.

While the other half expressed love and confidence in our leadership and denomination as a whole.

Dr. H. Stephen Shoemake of Louisville, relates a story he picked up. "A Texas rancher bought ten ranches and put them together into one big spread. His friend asked the name of the new ranch. The Texan replied, 'It's called the Circle Q, Rambling Brook, Double Bar, Broken Circle, Crooked Creek, Golden Horseshoe, Lazy B, Bent Arrow, Sleepy T, Triple O Ranch.' 'Wow!' the friend replied, 'I bet you have a lot of cattle.' ' No. Not many survive the branding.'

There is a temptation for us to "brand" each other negatively. But too much branding -- the Texan admitted--can reduce the herd."

Dear friend if we are to exist, an honest effort of cooperation must prevail at all levels and must be made by every preacher and layperson. Defiance and rebellion have no place in the ranks of Godly men. An attitude and spirit of animosity, suspicion, and pride will finally destroy a preacher, person, and place.

Cooperation enhances unity, to which I am committed.

In Matthew 20:20-24 please note the self-interest of James and John in desiring to sit one on each side of the Lord. Note also they sent their mother to do the job of asking Christ but further find in verse 24 the other ten disciples *"Were moved with indignation against the two brethren."*

We are at a crossroads and we need to take a lesson from John as we find him becoming the: TRUTH PRESENTER FROM SPIRITUAL IMPROVEMENT. There are two words that characterize John's later life and teaching. One is *love* and the other is *witness*. He uses the word LOVE more than eighty times and the word WITNESS in some form almost seventy times.

He becomes a real truth seeker. He was also borne out of the same zeal, passion and strength as was his brother James. He, like us had to work on loving his brothers. One phrase stands out from the mature John. *"My little children, love one another."*

It is not what you are that is important, but what you are willing to become.

May we learn to:

- Respect the person
- Resist pride
- Restore piety
- Re-examine our priority
- Refine by prayer
- Reform by practice

We come now to:

**The second group I call THE CONTENDERS - THE VARIED ONES -
- THE AUTOMATIC LEADERS.**

This type of leader is approachable. One should learn credibility is earned, not demanded.

Just as Simon is always first in the four listings, **PHILIP is thusly in this second four.** His name means "Lover of Horses." He was the skeptical, pessimistic, and analytical one. But the Lord uses men like this as well. Our churches and conferences are full of this type person. Men of caution, often visionless, but sometimes it is simply that they want to count the cost.

Philip like many was seeking to FIND HIS POTENTIAL. The first three gospels don't tell us anything about Philip. But John's gospel mentions him four times.

John 1:43-46: Where he is called to follow the Lord and where he leads Nathanael to Christ.

John 6:5-7: Where he was singled out by Christ relative to buying food for the 5,000. His response to Christ was, "We couldn't get 200 pennyworth from the whole crowd." What a shame to respond thusly when Jesus in verse 6 states why, *"And this He said to test him; for He knew himself what He would do."*

Philip was a materialist, methodical and mechanical. The type who would take out his pocket calculator and say, "We can't afford it!" He appears in the same three chapters as does Andrew but lacks the faith. He represents in part our stewardship program. We need to be unified in our denominational giving. We have never taught our people to give Biblically. A host of pastors don't tithe and multitudes of our members have never received the blessings or joy of giving. Our churches have been selfish. Therefore, due to the lack of outside giving has resulted in the withholding of God's blessing in every area of our denomination.

We need a Stewardship Commission to educate us. Or a stronger emphasis in our publications and colleges toward giving beyond our own local church to a total ministry.

Nearly every strong, virile denomination that is growing today has taught their people the value and blessing of unified giving.

Out of the top 10 giving states, 6 give through the unified co-op plan. An analyses revealed the fastest growing giving states were in this program. While it does not pay all the bills, those states involved were also the fastest growing toward quotas set by the departments and in establishing strong state and local agencies.

In the spirit of fairness however, it should be mentioned that other strong giving states exists who have not adopted this program.

Have we been against this program because of its author? The argument remains, but those who oppose enjoy spending the benefits none the less.

Also note the other two inclusions:

John 12:20-22. Here Philip brings the Greeks that come to him to Andrew who take them to Christ.

John 14:*8 "Lord show us the Father."* Many men like Philip have walked, led, sat where Christ is, but have yet to fully see the Father or Son. He followed Christ for over three years, but it is conceivable he represents so many yet today. However, he did have a seeking heart in the midst of his insecurity.

Now I come to BARTHOLOMEW **(NATHANAEL) the second in this grouping.**

Only one place tells us anything about him aside from the four lists and that is in John 1:46-51 where he is called Nathanael. Let us note here: HIS FLAW BECAUSE OF PREJUDICE.

He along with Philip, were students of the Scripture as noted in verse 45. But we see his sin when Nathanael was told about Jesus. He said, "Can anything good come out of Nazareth?"

In the recent survey it appeared many were saying, "Can anything good come out of Nashville?"

On a national level many sense: A lack of evangelistic thrust. Narrow scope for growth. Unwillingness to face the issues. Power struggle among departments. Leadership out of touch with the pastorate. Need new faces in old places. Place the Heavenly degree above the Nashville degree. Growth department catering just to large churches.

The more complimentary suggestions were: Need unity without uniformity. Return to Christian love.

Rekindle the old paths. Gear toward the small church to help them. Speak to our needs. Prepare correspondence courses for leaders-preachers. Literature improvement. Prepare literature for churches for growth. National ministers retreat.

PREJUDICE IS AN UNCALLED FOR GENERALIZATION BASED ON FEELINGS OF SUPERIORITY.

Prejudice is ugly in any form. It was prejudice that kept the Pharisees from responding because he wasn't from Jerusalem. They said of the apostles in Acts 2:7, 4:13 that they were ignorant, unlearned, Galilean hayseeds. Prejudice is used by Satan to blind people. However, I'm glad Nathanael's prejudice was not deep and we see,

Let's look at **HIS FAITH SEEN BY THE PHENOMENAL ONE**

*"Behold an Israelite indeed, in whom is no guile."* Verse 47. Thank God! That while prejudice exists among us, the tribe is dying. Like, Nathanael our knowledge of the Word is causing us to be less judgmental. May we be seekers of truth, not bound by prejudice, but honest, open, people of prayer.

Every child of God must one day stand before Christ to have his lifetime of service investigated.

Second Corinthians 5:10 states, *"We must all appear before the judgment seat of Christ; that every one may receive the things done in his body, according to that he hath done, whether it be good or bad."*

This judgment of believers is exclusively the responsibility of the Lord Jesus Christ. No mere mortal is capable of assuming the place of an omniscient, omnipotent God when it comes to judging men and movements. Finite human beings, regardless of their fundamental pedigree or position, are incapable of looking into another man's heart.

Only God can judge righteously. He said in Jeremiah 17:10, "I the Lord search the heart, I try the reins, even to give every man according to his ways, and according to the fruit of his doings.

This is why the Holy Spirit emphatically declares in Romans 14:4, 10-13: *"Who art thou that judgest another man's servant? to his own master he standeth or falleth. Yea, he shall be holden up: for God is able to make him stand...But why dost thou judge thy brother? or why dost thou set at nought thy brother? for we shall all stand before the judgment seat of Christ. For it is written, As I live, saith the Lord, every knee shall bow to me, and every tongue shall confess to God. So then every one of us shall give account of himself to God. Let us not therefore judge one another anymore: but judge this rather, that no man put a stumblingblock or an occasion to fall in his brother's way."*

We need to be careful about proclaiming and publishing the latest faults of brethren.

Remarks made against anyone are not worthy to be classified under the heading of 'defending the faith,' but rather as 'sowing discord among brothers,' a sin God adamantly hates (see Proverbs 6:16-19). Until the Lord is allowed to correct this terrible sin through a Holy Spirit-empowered revival of genuine love, our movement will decline and eventually die.

**A healthy body cannot exist without love.**

We come now to **MATTHEW is also known as LEVI.** It appears by his record he sees himself as THE WORST ONE of the disciple group.

The only picture we see of Matthew is found in three places (Matthew 9:9-13; Mark 2:14-17; Luke 5:27-32). It is the same incident--That of sitting at the seat of custom.

Look at **THE FAME FROM WHICH HE PROPELS.** He was a tax collector. However, he was willing to leave it entirely. Being a publican was not easy. It was even worse when you know the scriptures of y our fathers but not permitted in the temple because you were a Publican. There were outcast. Remember the publican who sat afar off and said, *"God be merciful to me a sinner."*

The Jewish Talmud said, "It is righteous to lie and steal from tax collectors." Matthew must have felt he was the worst one of the lot, because he alone in the listing of the twelve gives his occupation as a publican. The publicans were hated and despised by the Jewish society. Matthew in recording this is showing his genuine humility and expressing his sinful unworthiness.

While Matthew never speaks, never asks a question, never appears in another incident, his book is loaded with an appreciation for Christ.

Think **about THE FORGIVENESS HE PROPOSES.** Matthew 9:9-13, *"And as Jesus passed forth from thence, he saw a man, named Matthew, sitting at the receipt of custom: and he saith unto him, Follow me. And he arose, and followed him. And it came to pass, as Jesus sat at meat in the house, behold, many publicans and sinners came and sat down with him and his disciples. And when the Pharisees saw it, they said unto his disciples, Why eateth your Master with publicans and sinners? But when Jesus heard that, he said unto them, They that be whole need not a physician, but they that are sick. But go ye and learn what that meaneth, I will have mercy, and not sacrifice: for I am not come to call the righteous, but sinners to repentance."*

The theme of Matthew's message can in part be summed up in this same chapter as he asks which is greater, "to be saved from your sins or healed."

This book, called the Book of the King of Kings to the Jews, perhaps is so noted due to his including more Old Testament quotes of the Law and History than all the other gospels combined.

May I draw your attention to the distance he comes in order to follow Christ.

There were two classes of Tax collectors: The Gabbai and Mokhes. The Gabbai were the general collectors that collected property tax, income, poll tax, etc. The Mokhes collected duty and tolls on everything. They were divided into two groups. The Great Mokhes who hired others to do the collecting as he faded from sight and the little Mokhes who were too greedy to hire anyone else.

Matthew is saying I was a little Mokhes. I came from the table. I was saved from the undermost to the uttermost.

He like another publican (Zacheaus) did something no one else did after their conversion. They gave a banquet for their Saviour.

**Last in group two is THOMAS.** What do you think of when you think of Thomas? Doubter? If you do you may believe wrong. Perhaps he got bad press. Let us look at: **HIS FAITH WE DESIRE TO REPROVE.** In John 10:39 we find the account of where Jesus and the disciples had left Jerusalem because of the plot to take his life. But in John 11:14-16 the news of Lazarus's death is received and Jesus decides to return back to Bethany near Jerusalem. This caused a panic by the disciples except Thomas.

"Let us also go, that we may die with him." Verse 16b.

This is not characteristic of doubters but rather because he totally believed in Christ. John 14:1-5 *"Let not your heart be troubled: ye believe in God, believe also in me. In my Father's house are many mansions: if it were not so, I would have told you. And if I go and prepare a place for you, I will come again, and receive you unto myself; that where I am, there ye may be also. And whither I go ye know, and the way ye know. Thomas saith unto him, Lord, we know not whither thou goest; and how can we know the way?"*

Here he is saying, Lord don't you go somewhere we can't come. Thomas had a problem with separation. I don't like what I hear. You are going somewhere and we can't get there. We'll never find the place.

Jesus was crucified in John 19 and Thomas was destroyed. In John 20:24-29 we have the account of the disciples being gathered in the upper room after the crucifixion but Thomas was not there.

I knew it! He died and I didn't. I wanted to go with him and be where he is but he is gone.

He was depressed and had left the others who by the way were in the upper room "for fear."

Thomas was probably kicking every can in Jerusalem. He believed He was gone.

Before you label Thomas "the doubter" remember that none of the other disciples believed Jesus had risen until they saw him.

We should see Thomas in the light of John 20:29, *"Thou hast believed."* Here we see: HIS FIDELITY WE SHOULD REDUPLICATE.

Our faith and trust falters and our denomination needs to return to a stronger and deeper commitment to the Christ of our salvation.

We must take a look at our faith in what He wants to do in and through us.

We need to:
> Define our Purpose - that's Motive.
> Discover our Potential - that's Measure.
> Determine our Priorities - that's Manner.
> Direct our Program - that's Message.

Remember the Lord builds His church with:
> A Sanctified Preacher.
> A Separated People.
> A Salvaging Passion.
> A Saturating Program.

I am a denominational person owing my conversion to this movement, but frankly I'm not sure God is as thrilled that there is a Free Will Baptist denomination as I am. But, I am sure he is concerned about my indifference to the lost or my lack of reaching the lost here and around the world.

He is more concerned that people are saved than we continue as a denomination.

The reason any organization exists is to fulfill its preamble. If it wavers it has lost its reason to be. The responsibility is ours.

We may:
> Shirk it, because we are afraid to undertake it.
> Shelve it, because we are anxious to defer it.
> Shed it, because we are tired of hearing it.
> Or,

Shoulder it, because we are ready to fulfill it.
Share it, and be wise in distributing it.

Men or every level who are known as leaders but whose pride robs of true repentance can create a dike holding back the needful revival for themselves and those they influence. The streams of revival are held back when cold hearts continue to hold ill feelings.      We will never experience revival and restitution:

Until pastors and parishioners forgive each other.
Until churches and conference forgive each other.
Until states and leaders forgive each other.
Until every organization can say, I forgive!

When all our people: from President to pastor; leader to layman; can practice Matthew 18:15.

Then and only then will we move forward. Until we do, one must surely be fearful in saying, "let us go that we may die with him." How can He forgive us our trespasses when we don't? May the fountains of the Water of life, the Washing of regeneration once again flow and flood every member of our denomination.

### Group Three I call THE PRETENDERS -- THE VACILLATING ONE'S -- APPOINTED LEADERS

This third group represents a segment of our movement and they are many.

In many ways our people are suffering from a lack of good leadership. A vast number of our membership have a mistrust of denominational            affiliation            due            to misinformation. Communication falls rapidly from the National to the local church. Only about 8,000 receive Contact Magazine and maybe four times that amount receive *Mission-Grams* and *Heartbeat*. But this is far short of reaching the more than 200,000 members. We have 22 states publishing 22 different publications, but going to only about 42,000 people. Each defining or carrying the denominational message with their own bias.

A great transition exists today with a stronger emphasis being given to the local and state ministries. In fact, 22 states now have their own State Executive or Promotional Secretaries where the state and national programs are being promoted and with time a stronger program from the local conference to national convention will exist. Until then, national organizations would better their own programs by coordinating with these state leaders.

We now have 28 regular state conventions, 17 Free Will Baptist Bible Institutes in 10 states, 75 Christian schools in 22 states, 13 or so full-time evangelists, 4 colleges geographically centered across the United States, 9 National Boards and Commissions made up of 68 men and women, with 110 Foreign missionaries in 9 countries and 122 Home missionaries in 28 states and Canada, Mexico, Virgin Islands, and Puerto Rico. We also have chaplains serving in the Armed services.

Our statistics reveals we had 210 district associations, 2,598 churches and 213,025 members.

With plenty of prayer, preparation and a positive approach we can reach into every area of our denomination like never before.

Now let us look at these four disciples who always appear in this group. Just like our mass of people of whom we know so little, these disciples are the ones of whom we know only a little.

The first in Group three is **JAMES - THE SON OF ALPHASUS**. His name is always first in group three in all the four Biblical accounts.

The only thing the Bible tells us about this disciple is his name. He never says a word nor is spoken to but he is still one of the twelve. Because of this, let me address THE DESIGNATION HIS NAME PRESENTS.

In Mark 15:40 he is called *"James the Less."* The Greek word used in this title is "mikros" which means *little*. However, while it basically means "small in stature." Could it also mean "young in age" or "one of little influence?"

We may never know, but the Bible does tell us **SOME DETAILS OF HIS PEDIGREE.** Could Matthew have been his brother? According to Mark 2:14 Levi (Matthew) was also a son of Alphasus.

Could Jesus be his cousin? In John 19:25, "Now there stood by the cross of Jesus His mother, and His mother's sister, Mary the wife of Clopas..." Can we assume that no mother would name two daughters Mary and that she was actually a sister-in-law of Mary? Also, Clopas is another form of the name Alphasus. Is it possible that Alphasus as Joseph's brother making Christ and James cousins? To further substantiate this is Mark 15:40 where it refers to a Mary as *"The mother of James the Less."*

This James represents a vast multitude of our movement. There are thousands of people, mainly in leadership roles in churches and conferences, totally unknown outside his area. He is none the less their leader, and his influence, while little nationally or statewide, is followed locally. He is the overlooked person and is the person to be reached before the grassroots will ever be touched.

Be as it may, while not recognized outside his region, he like James will be recognized in Heaven. The Lord does use obscure, little, unknown, unsung men.

Secondly, **LEBBAEUS who is also known as JUDAS THADDAEUS.**

His name is THE **DEFINITION OF HIS PERSONALITY**. His name was Judas (Jehovah leads).

The names Lebbaeus and Thaddaeus may have been added at a later time to reflect his character.

Thadaeus comes from the Hebrew root *Thad*. It carries with it the meaning of being a "breast-child." He may have been the youngest child. The baby of the family. Lebbaeus comes from the Hebrew root *Leb,* which means "heart." A man of courage -- a heart-child.

What about **THE DECLARATION OF HIS PRIORITIES**. This man was also lost in obscurity but we find him one time in the scripture. John 14:21-24, "*He that hath my commandments, and keepeth them, he it is that loveth will manifest myself to him. Judas saith unto him, not Iscariot, Lord, how is it that thou wilt manifest thyself unto us, and not unto the world? Jesus* *answered and said unto him, If a man love me, he will keep my words: and my Father will love him, and we will come unto him, and make our abode with him. He that loveth me not keepeth not my sayings: and the word which ye hear is not mine, but the Father's which sent me."*

Jesus' answer simply put would be, "I can tell who loves me by the way they obey me. And only those who truly love me and obey me will I manifest myself to. The only people who will be able to perceive me are the ones who love me."

In other words, manifestation is limited to reception.

I believe ones dedication will be determined by:
The Master you serve.
The Message you share.
The Morals you sanction.
The Manners you show.

It was Bob Jones, Sr. who said, "The level of responsibility is determined by the level of opportunity."

A leadership with integrity does not wait to see what the trends are, or what is popular. The true leader sets the trends and rallies the people, even when the cause is unpopular.

How can the church remain silent when millions of unborn infants are being slaughtered?

How can the church remain silent when we are having an epidemic of divorce and are witnessing the breakdown of the family?

How can the church remain silent when racism has become sophisticated and hidden in political philosophy?

How can the church remain silent when there are those who are demanding that homosexuality be recognized as a valid Christian life style?

How can the church remain silent when our culture is drowning in a sea of alcohol? Where are the Carry Nations of our time?

What we know about **SIMON -- THE ZEALOT which means one JEALOUS FOR THE LAW.**

In Matthew and Mark, Simon is identified as "Simon the Canaanite."

Luke and Acts record him as "Simon, called Zealots." The Greek word used for Zelotes has the same meaning as the Hebrew root *quana* where the transliteration *Kananaios* is used.

The meaning of the words being "to be jealous."

Simon may have been identified with a party of Judaism known as the Zealots. His was one of the four dominant groups within Judaism! The Pharisees, Sadducees, Essenes, and the Zealots.

Think about THE DOCTRINE HE PRESENTED. The zealots were the most fervent, passionate, patriots of Judaism. Probably born out of the Maccabean period where Judas Maccabaeus led a revolt against Greek influences on the Jewish nation and religion. The intensity of the Zealot philosophy is seen in I Maccabees 2:50, *"Be ye zealous for the law and give your lives for the covenant."*

In New Testament times the Zealots fled to Masada after the destruction of Jerusalem led by a man named Eleazar. Here 960 zealots committed suicide rather than be taken by the hated Roman enemy according to Josephus, the Jewish historian (Wars of the Jews, book VII, Chapters VIII and IX).

Do you see **HIS DETERMINATION ABOVE HIS PARTNER?**
I believe that Simon's partner was Judas Iscariot as Jesus sent out the disciples two by two (Mark 6:7).

But Simon continued to believe and was transformed. Judas however fell short of the Mark.

I believe as Free Will Baptists we have failed to indoctrinate our people. We give up more people to denominations with a foreign biblical doctrine than we receive from others. I have observed many people join our churches across our denomination as I visit churches. Many were made members without having knowledge of our beliefs. Most didn't have the opportunity to even reject our covenant because it wasn't read to them. Many will never be taught our doctrine. That which made us what we are was a common belief and an abiding conviction about apostasy, feet washing, open communion, and local church autonomy, separating us from other denominations and their beliefs. These beliefs have been the chains that bind us together.

Many movements that are growing today are not side stepping doctrinal emphasis, but make it the center of their preaching along with salvation. The emphasis is on conversion, baptism, joining the local church, and living separated lives. Until we do this our losses will continue.

The last is **JUDAS ISCARIOT**. He always appears lasts in the groups listing.

The name Judas was a common one. Simply the Greek from of Judah-the land of God's people. Some say its root meaning is "Jehovah praised" but others "one who is the object of praise."

In any case it is sad that it was given to the one who rejects his Lord. Iscariot basically comes from a combination of the Hebrew term Ish, which means "man," and Kerioth, the name of a town. He was the "Man of Kerioth." He was Judas of Kerioth. In fact, he was the only disciple not from Galilee since Kerioth was in Judea near Hebron south of Jerusalem. Since he was not one of the acquaintances or brothers could it be he was never accepted as one of the group? However, he continues even from the beginning.

Remember Jesus demanded total commitment as early as John 6:66, *"From that time many of His disciples sent back, and walked no more with him."* Many left but the twelve stayed. Could he have been motivated by selfish purposes? What type of relationship did he have with Christ? Note what the scriptures say.

Psalm 41:9, *"Yea, mine own familiar friend in whom I trusted who did eat of my bread, hath lifted up his heel against me."*

Psalm 55:12-14, 20b-21, *"For it was not an enemy that reproached me; then I could have born it. Neither was it he that hated me that did magnify himself against me; then I would have hid myself from him: But it was thou, a man mine equal, my guide, and mine acquaintance. We took sweet counsel together, and walked unto the house of God in company...............he hath broken his covenant. The words of his mouth were smoother than butter, but war was in his heart: his words were softer than oil, yet were they drawn swords."*

Zechariah 11:12-13, *"And I said unto them, if ye think good, give me my price; and if not, forbear. So they weighed for my price thirty pieces of silver. And the Lord said unto me, cast it unto the potter: a goodly price that I was prised at of them. And I took the thirty pieces of silver, and cast them to the potter in the house of the Lord."*

John 17:12, "While I was with them in the world, I kept them in thy name: those that thou gavest me I have kept, and one of them is lost, but the son of perdition; that the scripture might be fulfilled."

Luke 22:21-22, *"But behold, the hand of him that betrayed me is with me on the table. And truly the Son of man goeth, as it was determined: but woe unto that man by whom he is betrayed!"*

Was it **HIS DESIRES DURING THE PRETENSE?** Judas never has a word to say until he complains about the money that Mary wasted in anointing Jesus' feet. This is the first time he speaks in the entire biblical record. John 12:3-6, *"Then took Mary a pound of ointment of spikenard, very costly, and anointed the feet of Jesus, and wiped his feet with her hair: and the house was filled with the odour of the ointment. Then saith one of his disciples, Judas Iscariot, Simon's son, which should betray him, Why was* *not this ointment sold for three hundred pence, and given to the poor? This he said, not that he cared for the poor; but because he was a thief, and had the bag, and bare what was put therein."*

REMEMBER THE SAME SUN THAT MELTS THE WAX HARDENS THE CLAY.

Was he the hypocrite of hypocrites? No one even suspected him. Outwardly, Judas appeared not to have a defective character. In fact, he was not even considered a betrayer right up to the last supper by his peers. When he left the upper room the other disciples thought he had only gone out to buy more food.

Judas had heard the same lessons as the other disciples.
The unjust steward (Luke 16:11-13).
The wedding garment (Matthew 22:11-14).
Lessons about money (Matthew 23:1-12).
Jesus even forewarned by saying in John 6:70b, *"One of you is a devil."* Even John 13:21, *"Verily, verily, I say unto you that one of you shall betray me."*

Was there a **DEPARTSURE HE PLANNED?** John 13:10b-11, 18-19, 21-29, *"He that is washed need not save to wash his feet, but is clean every whit: and ye are clean, but not all. For he knew who should betray him; therefore said he, ye are not all clean.....I speak not of you all: I know whom I have chosen: but that the scripture may be fulfilled, he that eateth bread with me hath lifted up his heel against me. Now I tell you before it come, that, when it is come to pass, ye may believe that I am he.....When Jesus had thus said, he was troubled in spirit, and testified, and said, Verily, verily, I say unto you , that one of you shall betray me. Then the disciples looked one on another, doubting of whom* he spake. *Now there was leaning on Jesus' bosom one of his disciples, whom Jesus loved. Simon Peter therefore beckoned to him, that he should ask who it should be of whom he spake. He then lying on Jesus' breast saith unto him, Lord, who is it? Jesus answered, He it is, to whom I shall give a sop, when I have dipped it. And when he had dipped the sop, he gave it to Judas Iscariot, the son of Simon. And after the sop Satan entered into him. Then said Jesus unto him, that thou doest, do quickly. Now no man at the table knew for what intent he spake this unto him. For some of them thought, because Judas had the bag, that Jesus had said unto him, buy those things that we have need of against the feast; or, that he should give something to the poor."*

Matthew26:16, *"And from that time he sought opportunity to betray him."*

Mark 14:11, *"And when they heard it, they were glad, and promised to give him money. And he sought how he might conveniently betray him."*

Luke 22:6, *"And he promised, and sought opportunity to betray him unto them in the absence of the multitude."*

John 18:2-4, *"And Judas also, which betrayed him, knew the place: for Jesus ofttimes resorted thither with his disciples. Judas then, having received a band of men and officers from the chief priests and Pharisees, cometh thither with lanterns and torches and weapons. Jesus therefore, knowing all things that should come upon him, went forth, and said unto them, whom seek ye?"*

Matthew 27:3,5, *"Then Judas, which had betrayed him, when he saw that he was condemned, repented himself, and brought again the thirty pieces of silver to the chief priests and elders. And he cast down the pieces of silver in the temple, and departed, and sent and hanged himself."*

Acts 1:18, "Now this man purchased a field with the reward of iniquity; and falling headlong, he burst asunder in the midst, and all his bowels gushed out."

Matthew 27:6-7, *"And the chief priests took the silver pieces, and said, it is not lawful for to put them into the treasury, because it is the price of blood. And they took counsel, and bought with them the potter's field, to bury strangers in."*

Acts 1:15-26, *"And in those days Peter stood up in the midst of the disciples, and said, (the number of names together were about an hundred and twenty.) Men and brethren, this scripture must needs have been fulfilled, which the Holy Ghost by the mouth of David spake before concerning Judas, which was guide to them that took Jesus. For he was numbered with us, and had obtained part of this ministry. Now this man purchased a field with the reward of iniquity; and falling headlong, he burst asunder in the midst, and all his bowels gushed out. And it was known unto all the dwellers at Jerusalem; insomuch as that field is called in their proper tongue, Aceldama, that is to say, The field of blood. For it is written in the book of Psalms, Let his habitation be desolate, and let no man dwell therein: and his bishoprick let another take. Wherefore of these men which have companied with us all the time that the Lord Jesus went in and out among us. Beginning from the baptism of John unto that same day that he was taken up from us, must one be ordained to be a witness with us of his resurrection. And they appointed two, Joseph called Barsabas, who was surnamed Justus, and Matthias. And they prayed, and said, Thou, Lord, which knowest the hearts of all men, shew whether of these two thou hast chosen. That he may take part of this ministry and apostleship, from which Judas by transgression fell, that he might go to his own place. Andy they gave forth their lots; and the lot fell upon Matthias; and he was numbered with the eleven apostles."*

Psalms 69:25-28, *"Let their habitation be desolate; and let thy wrathful anger take hold of them. Let their habitation be desolate; and let none dwell in their tents. For they persecute him who thou hast smitten; and they talk to the grief of those whom thou hast wounded. Add iniquity unto their iniquity: and let them not come into thy righteousness. Let them be blotted out of the book of the living, and not be written with the*

Judas represents those of our movement falling short of God's purpose for his life. Today we have a faltering family unit, pastors and laymen alike are falling speedily into the separation of the family. Many of our great and good men, preachers of the gospel, have become victims of divorce. Others are open prey for Satan's attack. It is advisable to remember Philip Brooks saying, "If God called you to preach, never stoop to be a king."

We need like never before a Family Life Commission and a strong emphasis on the Christian family in every area of our movement. It cannot be left to the clergy for they are hurting too and the church needs the message.

Teaching our people is one of our failings. Another is legalism. We seem to have the idea no better way exists than our own. With this type of attitude, our churches will cease to meet the needs of a changing society. I think most of our churches have reached the height of their growth. I don't think it's impossible for them to grow; I think it's improbable that they will. Therefore, if our denomination is to grow it will take new churches being organized. It will take men dedicated to the cause of growing a church for the cause of Christ.

Since there is a constant upward mobility involved in society as a whole, we need to strengthen, maintain, nourish, and develop our existing churches. We must open new churches for our children who are leaving our rural areas and going to cities, graduating from universities, becoming involved in industry. We cannot forget to serve every area of our changing society.

On a national level, we need to capitalize on what God had allowed us to have as denominational resources--our Bible College, Sunday school department, executive office, and mission departments. These departments are not mini-denominations with only their desire in mind. But we are one denomination with many organizations that need to remember we are one.

Our colleges need to produce men who are dedicated to our cause who believe we are a total denomination without prejudice to the uneducated or Non-bible College trained minister. Our mission departments should gear up in fulfilling the design of their organization with a cooperating spirit as the body advances. Our publications should foster unity in the body, and our curriculum press prepare material designed for edification.

All working together will provide the impetus we need for a unity which will produce growth.

The first Austrian to ever win a gold medal did so in the 1968 Olympics with a hand gun. He hit the bull's eye 100 times for a perfect score. Upon his return to Austria he was highly honored by his countrymen and sent out to inspire the youth. After the fanfare died he returned to his job. Only a short time later he lost his left hand in the machine at the plant he worked. Remembering the past he became quite discouraged. In fact, he was very hard to live with. One evening he came in pushing aside his wife and entered the bedroom where in the chest he found a pistol. His wife, knowing his deep despair, fell to her knees, paralyzed as she cried, "Oh, no." From the home he left crossing over the hillside. SHE SUDDENLY HEARD A BANG. Jumping to her feet she hastened and just as she hastened to the sound, just as she peered over the hillside, suddenly another bang. Bang. Bang. Bang.

In 1972 he won his second gold medal by hitting the bull's eye 99 out of 100 times.

He, while discouraged and despaired and crippled faltered, never lost his dream.

May we as Free Will Baptists not lose sight of our goal, our dream?

# 14

## Stewards of the Text

---

Delmar Sparks, Deceased
Founder Westerville Free Will Baptist Church

The Bible says that in the beginning God created. Thus starts the greatest story that has ever been told. The creation of man, how that God took from the dust of the earth—a handful of dirt, really--and molded man in His own image and breathed into his nostrils the breath of life. And the Bible said that he became a living soul and placed him in the garden. But man sinned and was separated from God. But God loved us and began to work a redemption plan whereby we could be redeemed by His love. Not what we are, but by His love. And thus the 66 books and the 40 writers—the greatest book that has ever been written. And this book closes with even so come, Lord Jesus. May the grace of God be with you all. From the very first, the first five words that in the beginning that God created to the last in the book of Revelation, we are the stewards of the text—and that's my assignment tonight and I appreciate it.

We are charged with this stewardship. God is immutable. God's Word does not change. We need the assurance of this not only as John told us in his writing, "These things have I written to you who believe, that you may know that ye have eternal life." We need the assurance that we get from the Word of God and the promises. Someone suggested at the Bible Conference taking all of his best points from his messages and preaching them. And I've considered taking all the best points I've heard since I've come here and preaching them, because there have been some beautiful things that have been said—some beautiful teachings from the Word of God. But the old hymn writer has said, "How firm a foundation, ye saints of the Lord, is laid for your faith in his excellent word. What more can he say than to you he hath said, to you who for refuge to Jesus have fled."

We have the story of a farmer who had been saved but really lacked assurance. And he asked God for a sign. And he said "Lord, if I have really been saved then over in this corner of the field place ten sheep when I go over there this afternoon." And he went, and sure enough, there was ten sheep over there. Boy, he was happy...for a little while. And it dawned on him that perhaps it was just a coincidence. And so he said, "Now Lord, have ten other sheep in a different place for my assurance." And he anxiously went later and sure enough there were ten sheep there. Someone asked him, "Did this give you assurance?" and he said "No. Nothing gave me certainty until I got the sure Word of God." And that's what we need to base it on folks. It doesn't make any difference if we have formal training of not, I want us to look at this.

Jeremiah—God spoke to him and said that he was going to destroy Jerusalem, and the king was perturbed about what

Jeremiah had said. And the king did not want to hear that. And he sent a little later for Jeremiah and asked, "Is there any word from the Lord?" Jeremiah said, "There is, but it's the same word. The word from God has not changed any." Formal training or not, we can be faithful. Most scholars agree that the teachings of Jesus on the 3

What we are is the product of the faithfulness of others. I remember that in my childhood the preachers that I so respected, now I won't get off on a tangent to try to express the respect we should have for them. How they lived was as important at influencing me as what they said. As a teenager growing up, sometimes we see young Christians and they don't know what to do so they do what they see others doing. And we need to set the example for them. They after a while will learn to give and forgive and they will learn to do it for the right reasons and with the right attitude. We on the local level, we must give our attention to producing Sunday school teachers, youth workers, CTS...building strong and not necessarily big churches, local churches. The package is not what gets the job done, it's the product in the package. What we see tonight represents progress in numbers. We have come a long way.

I sat there tonight and I remember as a pre-teen at the mouth of Cam Creek sat Elizabeth tabernacle with sawdust floors, coal oil lamps, and great revivals. And God is still the same today. His Word is still the same today. We have made progress, and praise God for that. We have made progress in numbers, education—Sunday school, CTS, methods and presentation--but we must have progress in our spiritual development. Regeneration changes our nature. The day I got saved, there was something that changed in my life. I used to take my wife to church and then sit in the church yard and read the Sunday morning paper---didn't bother to go inside. But the day God changed my life, I could not wait to get back to church that night. Regeneration changes our nature. Justification changes our standing. Sanctification changes our character. And that's what we are. That's what we must develop in our lives. If we're going to make progress, then that's what we must do as we study and apply the Word of God to our lives. The foundation has been laid. I'm convinced of that—we have a solid foundation, and Jesus Christ is that foundation. The potential is there—in the Sunday school, pews, and homes. The personnel is there. The power is available. The progress is up to us. For the stewardship to progress, we must know and apply the Word of God. It's not enough just to know. We must apply it to our lives.

Let me show you what John says, I John 3:2-3 (quotes). And I believe that's moving forward, and growing in the grace and the knowledge of our Lord and Savior Jesus Christ. Some grains of wheat were found, thousands of years old, but they hadn't produced anything. They had not been planted. They had not been watered. And the scripture teaches that one sows, another waters, but God gives the increase. I never saved a soul in my life. God gives the increase if we know and apply the Word of God. He's promised. The stewardship of the text can only be fulfilled by the power of the Holy Spirit. Acts 1:8.

In Acts 19, we have some recordings of some apostate Jews who had heard the message and seen Paul cast out demons and they thought they would do it also. They tried to cast out this evil spirit, and the evil spirit said, "Jesus I know, and Paul I know, but who are you?" The power of the Holy Spirit is the difference. It says the Word of God is quick and powerful and sharper than any two-edged sword. The apostle Paul, writing to the church of Ephesus, told them to put on the whole armor of God. He said to take the sword of the Spirit which is the Word of God. We have it in our hands, we must have it in our hearts. The weapons of our warfare are not carnal. They are mighty through God for pulling down the strongholds of the devil. The Word of God—quick and powerful, able to do exceeding abundantly more than we think it can do. We must not handle it deceitfully. We must live it.

I remember as a young Christian, seeing a local church sign that said don't do as I do, do as I say. That always stuck with me. I'll tell you—could I insert here—I know that God in one sense that God requires the same of us as He requires of everyone else. But there is something different about a preacher—God has laid His hand on us. Paul instructs us in Timothy to live to a higher standard (I Timothy 4). Be an example unto the believer. And he didn't just leave it in generalities, he put some specifics in there. In words, we need to be careful of the words that we use. In word, in conversation, in our everyday conduct of our lives. I believe that people ought to see that there is something different about us. I believe the preacher ought to set the example.

I Corinthians 13:4—charity is long suffering and is kind. Be thou an example in purity. Where is your mind? You don't have to water, plow and harvest those thoughts. Get them out. That's what he was talking about—purity. Paul said, "Give thyself wholly to them, that thy profiting may appear to all." In II Timothy, the preaching. If we are to have power in our preaching and stewardship, we must spend time in prayer and study. That's one of the things I've wrestled with. I was raised on a farm, and all I knew was hard work. It was difficult to reprogram my brain that it was okay to sit in an air conditioned office and meditate, study, pray, and agonize with God for my people. I believe that's a part of our responsibility. We must live holy lives allowing God to speak to us. If we are charged with the stewardship of the Word, we are charged with the purity of the Word. Preach the Word. We must not change the Word to fit '89. We must change '89 to fit the Word. If our text becomes tinted, our progress is impeded and our product is flawed. The Word sanctifies, sets us apart, and cleans us up. Jesus prayed sanctify them through your truth, thy word is truth. The word have I hid in my heart that I might not sin against thee. I want to have that word in there.

The stewardship of the Word is not confined to just preachers—the deacons, the Sunday school teachers, the CTS, the youth, and the home. We are all charged with the responsibility of the stewardship of the Word. And so Paul instructs Timothy in I Timothy and II Timothy, he said preach the Word. That's what we need to do. There is nothing else that will get the job done. There are other things that will help and assist, but the Word is the only thing that will get the job done.

In I Corinthians 2:1-5, Paul gives us an outline for the preaching of our text, for the preaching of the Word of God. The three points are: the message, the method, and the motive for our preaching the Word of God. Paul did not only preach a Jesus of Galilee, he preached one of Calvary. Paul said in I Corinthians 1:17, Christ sent me not to baptize but to preach the gospel. Not with wisdom of words, lest the cross of Christ should be made of non-effect. The preaching of the cross. I Corinthians 15, Paul defined what the gospel is—the death, burial, and resurrection of the Lord Jesus Christ. Now Paul tells us in verse 14 what five things will be the result if Jesus did not raise from the dead. If Christ be not risen, there is no resurrection; if there is no resurrection, our preaching is in vain. He said your faith is also vain. If Jesus did not raise from the dead, our faith is in vain. We have nothing to cling to. The third thing, we are false witnesses because we testified that God raised him from the dead. But if there be no resurrection of the dead then Christ be not risen.

And then he goes on and says ye are yet in your sins. That's the fourth thing. People say Free Will Baptists have no security. I've never considered going back on the Lord. But I'll tell you one of the most sobering thoughts I've ever had—to stand in the presence of the Almighty God and give an account of my stewardship. If Jesus has not risen from the dead, we are yet in our sins; and those who are asleep in him are perished, if there be no resurrection of the dead. If in this life only we have hope in Christ we are of all men most miserable. It is great to live for the Lord and He does bless us. But if there is no resurrection of the dead, we have no hope past death's door. Terrible, terrible thought.

Then this is the message. The message is the death, burial, and resurrection of the Lord Jesus Christ. The method in verse 4 says and my speech and my preaching was not with enticing words of men's wisdom but in demonstration of the Spirit. Paul was not concerned with impressing men that he might take an ego trip. Paul was concerned with preaching the Word, that there would be power when he preached. And power comes from holy living. Power comes from head and heart preparation. If we are going to preach and teach, then we need to prepare our head by study and research and we need to prepare our heart by being in prayer to God. We need to have a close fellowship with God. The most powerful charge I've ever heard given to a young man being ordained—they thrust the Bible at him and said here is a gold mine...dig it out. But do you know what? In this day of instant everything, that's tough. A lot goes into preparation.

Verse 5 says, that your faith should not stand in the wisdom of men but in the power of God. Why do you preach? Why do you teach? For the name? For the job? Paul desired that the people would stand in the right thing that was his goal and ambition. People must stand in the power of God not in the preacher...not in the local church...not in other people. Floods will come that you cannot control. There will be rivers that you can't cross. Mountains that you can't climb. Valleys that you can't cross. But God can. God said I'll never leave you and I'll never forsake you. Hang your hat on that promise. And God will never leave you.

Two motives for preaching: that people might be saved. Paul desired to see people saved. The second thing was spiritual maturing. Hebrews 6—therefore leaving the principles of the doctrine of Christ let us go on to perfection. Let us go on to completion. Paul wrote to the church of Ephesus in 4:8 (quoted). In verse 11-13 (quoted). If there's to be power, progress, and preaching and it's going to produce, this is what it is going to produce. Verse 14-16 (quoted), the product. Will the product of a bygone generation and what we are...I'm hoping others will come along and build on the foundation that we have built on and go forward to the glory of God.

# 15

## "Finding Your Vision at the Well"
### John 4:4-42

Louis Nettleton
Williams Road Free Will Baptist Church

### Beginnings

Traditionally this passage of scripture is preached with a heavy emphasis on Evangelism, and rightfully I might add, but I also see divine appointments being set, not just for the woman at the well, but the Disciples, the town's people, all being gather by Jesus at the Jacob's well. There each person or group was to receive a special touch from the Messiah. Jewish tradition speaks of the well as being dug by Jacob to bring peace in the battle over water. With a well to the East and other to the North prior to Jacob's Well Tribes battled over the use and amounts of water which brought much despair. With Jacob digging the well somewhat in the middle of these two wells is it relieved the pressure over the water issues bringing peace in the battle over the much needed water. This well of Jacob not only brought life but first brought peace.

Jesus arrives at the well with history in hand using it to set up a Divine Intersection to proclaim himself the Messiah, and thus being the Messiah able to transcend the physical and spiritual realms using the water of Jacob's well to be HIS object lesson. At the well He would be able to use the physical properties of the water to teach the limited effects it has on our bodies and the need to keep indulging to maintain its effect upon our flesh but in contrast the Living Water of the Messiah would be able to give eternal life satisfying spiritual needs for eternity. It is the Living Water that satisfies our souls freeing us from the imprisonment of our flesh that constantly cries out more! More! Never satisfied, leaving us in failure, neglect, feeling unloved, forgotten, abused, and demeaned.

When Jesus speaks HE always has a destination in mind. HE never speaks into our lives without having an eternal destination and an earthly place to drive home our worth through the grace of God. It is our self-centeredness that causes us to miss the place God has in mind for us to be used of HIM touching others, bringing peace, fulfillment, and satisfaction, into our being. We assume God desire to satisfy our fleshly needs and we interpret God through the limiting effects of our flesh never coming to grips with what God is or what HE truly desires. We struggle to live our lives feeling as if success is just beyond our reach. We begin to question God and if not God then our self-worth when this happens we begin to act like the Pharisees pursuing meaningless adventures to build a false sense of worth and righteousness we go out of way to keep from getting our hands dirty with the sin of this world, elevating ourselves as if we are better than those trapped in sin's darkness. We create ways around the undesirables just like the Pharisees so we don't have to deal with them.

## The Messiah

**John 4:4**, "And HE must need go through Samaria. KJV
**John 4:4**, "It was necessary for HIM to go through Samaria." AMP

When I look at the language of the original text I believe that Jesus had a purpose in mind, a vision for ministry a life altering message to be delivered. HIS vision required a sacrifice, a three day journey to bring salvation to confused souls. I find it so deeply intriguing that Jesus takes a journey that would take HIM in the territory rejected by the Priest and Pharisees to a people rejected by the Jews for being half breeds dating back to the rebuilding of Jerusalem in Nehemiah's time and that the journey was three days when Jesus springs forth form the ground like an eternal spring of water offering the hope of eternal life.

Christ vision given to HIM via the Father required a sacrifice and it is no different for you and me! God is in the business of giving us a vision for ministry, a vision that provides hope for justice in an unjust World but not without a sacrifice. Americans have grown lazy and indifferent to God's call to affect society with the message of the Gospel. This show up in the lack of concern for the oppressed, our overall lack of giving to the physical needs of the Body, and the attitude of malaise in regard to obedience to the Word of God. In our need for sacrifice our pharisaical lifestyle shows up excusing ourselves from such. I personally believe this is the reason so many Churches are failing today. Are we not to sacrifice our bodies a living sacrifice upon to God which is the base line of service. Vision is not apprehended without offering a sacrifice of time, money, or effort. Embrace the vision to touch your neighbors, co-workers, and family with the gospel the Water of Life.

Jesus goes to the Well to set up a Divine appointment for a Samaritan woman, the Disciples, and a town. For the Samaritan woman the stage was being set for a mind altering, life changing experience. For the Disciples the stage was being set for a Divine lesson of purpose and grace. Then for the town's people the stage was being set to receive a rejected people. This is not the end to this historical setting one very important lesson is being taught to you and I and that is the method Jesus uses to one woman and seeing her testimony multiplying the effect of Grace. Jesus also makes HIS humanity know by allowing HIS humanity to be seen by thirsting this pts HIM on the same level as the woman even submitting to her and drinking water she had gathered for HIM **(John 4:6)** Jesus was more than willing to touch the untouchable bringing her the opportunity to experience the life changing effects of Grace.

Vision is never about you but about others who are in need of the Savior's touch. We become a vehicle of Grace allowing God to pour through us into the hearts and minds of those in need thus multiplying the effect of Grace.

**The Disciples**

**John 4:8**, (For the disciples were gone away unto a city to buy meat.) KJV
**John 4:8**, "For HIS disciples had gone off into the town to buy food." AMP

There isn't anything wrong with the disciples going to buy food but it seems short sighted to me that Jesus being the Messiah would not be able to meet there needs if they had not gone into town but stayed with Jesus. When we find ourselves wondering away from Jesus we get in trouble. One of the consistent problems of the disciples was to see beyond physical needs limiting their understanding of the power of Jesus keeping them from discovering experiencing their own Divine vision leading deeper into faith trusting God supply their needs. I believe the Disciples here reflect misguided spiritual leaders. Just today I was talking a Godly man and his comment about failing churches was rooted in a lack of Spiritual leadership and I agree! Many Church leaders cast their vision into meaningless adventures in an attempt to feel worthy of their calling. I see many men of God laboring in the flesh preparing task and deeds instead of praying long and deeply over the issues in front of him. I firmly believe that when the congregants rule the Church the Pastor is caught begin the will of the people verses the will of God. I believe it is clear Biblical leadership is a Theocracy. I see many Churches casting their fleshly interpretation of vision over the man of God binding him thus making him ineffective unable to lead. I can't help but believe we act more like Pharisees than we care to admit. When we glorify our misguided adventures as measures of our righteousness we no longer are able to see God's vision for our lives let alone the Church.

**John 4:27**, "And upon this came his disciples, and marvelled that he talked with the woman: yet no man said, What seekest thou? or, Why talkest thou with her?" KJV
**John 4:27**, "Just then His disciples came, and they were surprised to find Him talking with a woman. However, no one said, "Why are You talking to her?" AMP

They seem to hold the food mission as important if not more important than the Samaritan woman. They had food for their Master and they knew HE is hungry and this woman should get out of their way, but they did not speak this out loud. How often do we elevation our ideals our jobs or our reasoning above everyone else? This is not vision it is nothing more than misguided adventures based on our selfish desires. The disciples at this time felt nothing was as important than feeding Jesus after all we have to eat to live... Right? Don't we do the same thing, for example, over the course of my ministry I have heard countless people say things like, "I can't come to Church I have to work". If you really thought God and Church were important wouldn't you find a job that would allow you to attend or wouldn't you downgrading your lifestyle so you could take a lesser paying job to put God first and foremost in your life? How about this, family reunions, or family coming into town and you put God in the back seat putting your family in the front seat missing Church. We have grown to diminish the importance of Church elevating our fleshly desires. I am so thankful for my Dad who taught me the value of family and that family never outweighs God.

**John 4:31**, In the mean while his disciples prayed him, saying, Master, eat. 32 But he said unto them, I have meat to eat that ye know not of. 33 Therefore said the disciples one to another, Hath any man brought him ought to eat? 34 Jesus saith unto them, My meat is to do the will of him that sent me, and to finish his work. 35 Say not ye, There are yet four months, and then cometh harvest? Behold, I say unto you, Lift up your eyes, and look on the fields; for they are white already to harvest. 36 And he that reapeth receiveth wages, and gathereth fruit unto life eternal: that both he that soweth and he that reapeth may rejoice together. 37 And herein is that saying true, One soweth, and another reapeth. 38 I sent you to reap that whereon ye bestowed no labour: other men laboured, and ye are entered into their labours. KJV

**John 4: 31**, Meanwhile, the disciples were urging Jesus [to have a meal], saying, "Rabbi (Teacher), eat." 32 But He told them, "I have food to eat that you do not know about." 33 So the disciples said to one another, "Has anyone brought Him something to eat?" 34 Jesus said to them, "My food is to do the will of Him who sent Me and to completely finish His work. 35 Do you not say, 'It is still four months until the harvest comes?' Look, I say to you, raise your eyes and look at the fields and see, they are white for harvest. 36 Already the reaper is receiving his wages and he is gathering fruit for eternal life; so that he who plants and he who reaps may rejoice together. 37 For in this case the saying is true, 'One [person] sows and another reaps.' 38 I sent you to reap [a crop] for which you have not worked. Others have worked and you have been privileged to reap the results of their work." AMP

Even after seeing Jesus busy with the Woman the Disciples seem to set on the physical wanting Jesus to eat so that their mission of bringing food to HIM would be validated. I fear finding myself heaped in busy work and missing the vision God. My vision, our leadership vision is to teach you the world of God to lead you reaching into the darkness of this World and by the grace of God giving souls trapped in that darkness hope everlasting found in the sacrifice of Jesus. In order to maintain this vision I am regularly making sacrifices in every area of my life and in doing so I have never been happier. I cannot let myself be bogged down in endless works of my hands ignoring the call of my Divine vision. God is calling us all to go deeper and deeper into HIS Grace fulfilling the Divine vision planted in each of our hearts. I am challenging each of you make sacrifices of your time money and effort to rise to the call of God. God is never satisfied with our idleness. Don't sit idle letting circumstances cast your vision to do so is to be imprisoned in the lies of Satan. Much of the Church is satisfied being reactionary instead of taking the glory of God into the darkness of its community.

It seemed to be alright to go into the city a Samaritan city and get what they felt they needed but they questioned at least in their minds why was Jesus talking to a Samaritan woman let alone sharing a cup of water. Too many Christian see themselves as good soil and everyone else as bad soil justifying idleness. Some leaders idolize their idleness with the misadventure of edification... I will let that sink in for a second. I contend that true Edification cannot take place in the safety of the local Church it requires the sacrifice and danger of reaching into the darkness!

Many Churches have avoided the difficult becoming satisfied with Spiritual poverty in fact some glorify their poverty. I meet Pastors and Leaders who seemingly don't want to get their hands dirty by touching the least, the lost, the imprisoned, the enslaved, and the hurting. In times past I have told others of taking in a young woman trapped in the darkness of addiction and their reply is, "I would never think of doing such a thing!" I reply, "You have lost sight of your vision." Many Church members never think about reaching those trapped in woeful condition of sin yet the Bible speaks over and over of the need every believer has to reach out rescuing as many souls as we can. We sit back on our pews or chairs in our sanctuaries waiting for the imprisoned soul to wonder into our buildings. I have found that people who are busy reaching out rescuing souls don't have time to complain. This where the Disciples are made to realize their misadventure for food paled in comparison to the vision Jesus was casting over them as they laid their eyes upon a field white unto harvest.

### The Samaritan Woman

**John 4:16**, "Jesus saith unto her, Go, call thy husband, and come hither. 17 The woman answered and said, I have no husband. Jesus said unto her, Thou hast well said, I have no husband: 18 For thou hast had five husbands; and he whom thou now hast is not thy husband: in that saidst thou truly." KJV
**John 4:16**, At this, Jesus said, "Go, call your husband and come back." 17 The woman answered, "I do not have a husband." Jesus said to her, "You have correctly said, 'I do not have a husband'; 18 for you have had five husbands, and the man you are now living with is not your [f]husband. You have said this truthfully." AMP

I believe Grace is all about us enabling us to live life the just and unjust when given a choice to pay attention to God's Grace or move forward under our own strength we increasingly choose our own strength. I see the Samaritan Woman as a representative of the human race. Her woeful condition is but a reflection of our own sinful condition. The contrast of the water being physical verses the Living Water is a picture of the earthly kingdom in contrast to the Kingdom of God. God's creation has always had this choice and throughout Biblical history time and time again we see mankind choosing physical strength over Spiritual power.

Another thought on the contrast issue what we see is not always the truth or the best verses the truth of what we don't see but none the less is the best. The woman knew the value of the physical water but was not considering the Spiritual water let alone her need for this unseen water. This is the struggle people face every day they are eager to embrace the perceived beauty of another only to find the ugliness of selfish behavior buried within. Our society has fixed their eyes on the physical creating a lifestyle ruled by its sensual desires. They allow their fleshly desires to usurp the validity of the Bible never considering the power of the unseen. This sensual perspective is one of the leading reasons people or running away from the Bible into the arms of s sin limited religion called Humanism.

The Samaritan woman had been married five times and currently was living with the sixth man in her adult life. Not seeing it at that very moment the sixth man of her physical life was being contrasted by a seventh man that could set straight all the errors of her past. Yet in HIS presents she seeks to evade the depth of her sin by redirecting the subject matter to errant Theology. I believe this speak louder than any other part of this passage. I confront people on a daily basis that wants to make up errant doctrines that lead them to blame God or the Church for the ills of society. If you cannot beat them then blame them! Our vision should be on Jesus digging out truth from the Word of God not relying on second hand Theology. I believe the local Church is responsible to not just proclaim the truth but to lead people deep into the doctrines of the Bible producing mature Christian engaging the darkness. Much of the Gospel is to be dug out when we do so our belief/faith is strengthened making it much harder to lead astray.

**John 4:28**, The woman then left her water pot, and went her way into the city, and saith to the men, 29 Come, see a man, which told me all things that ever I did: is not this the Christ? 30 Then they went out of the city, and came unto him. KJV
**John 4:28**, Then the woman left her water jar and went into the city and began telling the people, 29 "Come, see a man who told me all the things that I have done! Can this be the Christ (the Messiah, the Anointed)?" 30 So the people left the city and were coming to Him. AMP

The Samaritan woman sees Jesus as the Messiah and HE leads her past the objections, the bad Theology, and past the second hand doctrines finding salvation. In verse 28, you find these words, "The woman then left her water pot..." Leaving the physical water behind she set her eyes on her newly found vision, to tell the story of the Messiah at the well, which leads me to say, "What good is your maturity if your maturity doesn't penetrate the darkness rescuing other imprisoned souls." The vision here is not just one person or one family but a town!

**The Well**

**John 4:6**, "Now Jacob's well was there. Jesus therefore, being wearied with his journey, sat thus on the well..." KJV
**John 4:6**, "Jacob's well was there. So Jesus, tired as He was from His journey, sat down by the well..." AMP

I love it when God connects the new with the old adding validity to the overall message of the Bible. Here at Jacob's well the present is connected to a past that had special meaning to the Samaritans. This connection takes us back to before the Egyptian enslavement to Joseph's time when he was hated by his brethren sold into slavery ending up in Egypt. The area that belongs to the

Samaritan people was the inheritance of Joseph's sons Manasseh and Ephraim. When it came time for Jacob to bestow the family blessing Joseph aligns Manasseh on the right of Jacob and Ephraim on the left this would allow Manasseh the eldest to receive the right hand of Jacob as the leader of the future but Jacob crosses his hands placing his right hand upon Ephraim making him the future of the family and Manasseh his servant. Jacob had received the family blessing from Isaac and now the younger once again receives the blessing. Jesus leaves Judea early in HIS ministry to travel into a forbidden land to touch a despised people at Jacob's well. God has a history of taking the least and making them the best. God is using Jacob's well a respected place both in the Southern and Northern areas of Israel and teaching that the least will be the first. Jesus was not about to ignore the people of Samaria it seems to me that Joseph was still being rejected by his brothers.

I believe that Jacob's well, at least for our time, is the Church, at the well people were taught purpose, given hope, and rescued from darkness of neglect. Jesus being at the well is a reflection of Jesus in us and in our Churches and through the Church He is trying to activate a vision in each heart pouring Divine Grace through us into those captivated by the darkness of this World. The local church is a place where God leads people for a divine intersection with God/Holy Spirit bringing souls to salvation.

Your vision is not about you or your selfish desire it's about Jesus! If your vision is not cast towards souls trapped in the darkness of sin then I dare say you are living in selfishness not surrender. Too often we want to connect our vision to our perceived needs only to find that we are frustrating the work of the Holy Spirit that seeks to instill a Godly vision within us expecting us to trust in God to meet all our needs.

Our Church is not here to make you comfortable! We are not here to smooth over your rough edges tickling your ears and making you feel better but to stir you up and send you out to touch hurting souls. Church is not about comfort but forgiveness! We seem to be looking for the wrongs things when we go to Church much like the Samaritan woman. In **John 4:10**, Jesus answered and said unto her, If thou knewest the gift of God, and who it is that saith to thee, Give me to drink; thou wouldest have asked of him, and he would have given thee living water.

11 The woman saith unto him, Sir, thou hast nothing to draw with, and the well is deep: from whence then hast thou that living water? This woman was at this point unable to comprehend the message of Living Water declaring HE (Jesus) had bucket to draw water. Listen never under estimate the power of Jesus to pull out of thin air all our needs. I would suggest that mankind's problem is his difficulty to trust in God instead of taking great joy and worth in laboring or reasoning yourself out of trouble.

www.ingramcontent.com/pod-product-compliance
Lightning Source LLC
Chambersburg PA
CBHW061724020426
42331CB00006B/1082

* 9 781940 609331 *